The Politics of Being Afro-Latino/Latina

The Politics of Being Afro-Latino/Latina

Ethnicity, Colorism, and Political Representation in Washington, D.C.

Isreal G. Mallard

LEXINGTON BOOKS
Lanham • Boulder • New York • London

Published by Lexington Books
An imprint of The Rowman & Littlefield Publishing Group, Inc.
4501 Forbes Boulevard, Suite 200, Lanham, Maryland 20706
www.rowman.com

86-90 Paul Street, London EC2A 4NE

Copyright © 2022 by The Rowman & Littlefield Publishing Group, Inc.

All rights reserved. No part of this book may be reproduced in any form or by any electronic or mechanical means, including information storage and retrieval systems, without written permission from the publisher, except by a reviewer who may quote passages in a review.

British Library Cataloguing in Publication Information Available

Library of Congress Cataloging-in-Publication Data

ISBN 978-1-66690-817-6 (cloth)
ISBN 978-1-66690-819-0 (paperback)
ISBN 978-1-66690-818-3 (electronic)

*To my parents, Ira George and Cassie B. Mallard.
"I can do all things through Christ who strengthens me."*

Contents

List of Figures	ix
List of Tables	xi
Acknowledgments	xiii
Introduction	1
Chapter 1: Background	13
Chapter 2: Competing Perspectives	25
Chapter 3: Afro-Latino/a Identity and Electability	51
Chapter 4: Pathways to Political Office	73
Chapter 5: Summary, Conclusions, and Policy Recommendations	89
Bibliography	97
Index	105
About the Author	109

List of Figures

Figure 0.1: Conceptual Framework of the Ability for Afro-Latinos/as to Achieve Public Office

Figure 1.1: Hispanic Racial Demographics in Washington, DC

Figure 1.2: Racial Demographics in Washington, DC

List of Tables

Table 1.1: Ethnic Composition in Washington, DC
Table 3.1: Interview Participants

Acknowledgments

A book of this kind is essentially, in some sense, a work of collaboration. As a scholar in political science, I have drawn on the labors of others in this academic field. To them I owe a debt and with humbleness, I express my gratitude.

Among my family, I am particularly grateful to my sisters Caprice, Sharvete, and Sharmira who have been my strongest supporters since I begin this project. I thank my brothers Idol, Ivan and Iron as well as Miariah, Michyra and Zion for their moral support.

I am particularly grateful to Dr. Clement A. Akassi for his patience and for supporting me through this project. Also, I'm indebted to Dr. Abdul Karim Bangura who has played an integral role in my academic development.

My friends, Dr. Joshua Daspit, Dr. Elan Mitchell-Gee and Dr. Brian Easley who have been a constant support and to them I express my thankfulness. To the participants in my research and contributors to this study, thank you.

Introduction

This chapter introduces the purpose of this study and provides the problem statement and major research questions for this book. Also, this chapter provides the reader with the major research questions and hypotheses. In addition, the methodology, conceptual framework, theoretical framework will be examined in this book. Lastly, the chapter will cover the data collection, sampling techniques, and data sources as well as the data analytical techniques and the organization of the rest of this book.

For starters, this study attempts to analyze the political underrepresentation of Afro-Latinos/as in the District of Columbia (DC). The main objective of this book is therefore to identify presumed factors that influence the socio-political attitudes of Afro-Latino/a voters and how colorism plays a role in the Afro-Latino/a community. Thus, the study seeks answers to the following questions: What social/racial factors influence the electability of light-skin and dark-skin self-identified Afro-Latinos/as running for political office in Washington, DC? How do social/racial factors influence the pathway to political office for self-identified Afro-Latinos/as?

Next, a part of this project is aimed to identify if and how skin-color of Afro-Latinos/as impacts the likelihood of gaining access to public office. In-depth interviews were conducted with Latinos/as of African descent of different phenotypes who live in the District of Columbia. This research identifies and analyzes contributing factors that help to explain the virtual non-existence of Afro-Latinos/as as political representatives in elected or appointed offices in the District of Columbia.

Also, although there have not been many self-identified Afro-Latinos/as to be elected to public office in DC government, many Afro-Latinos/as in the area have served in some capacity throughout the government. Many examples illustrate the presence of Afro-Latinos/as in high profile government positions that began to emerge within the last 25 years. This development is important because it provides a setting for which to examine the potential for Afro-Latinos/as to enter public office in DC.

In addition, in the judicial branch of government, two Afro-Latino judges who were confirmed in the 1990s are the Honorable Ricardo Urbina and the Honorable José M. López. Judge Ricardo Urbina was nominated by former President Bill Clinton and confirmed by the Senate on June 15, 1994. The Honorable José M. López was appointed to the Superior Court of the District of Columbia in 1990 by President George H. Bush and currently serves as the Presiding Judge of the Domestic Violence Unit.

Furthermore, in local government, many members of the Afro-Latino/a community classify former DC Mayor Adrian Fenty as the District of Columbia's first Afro-Latino Mayor. Mr. Fenty, whose father is originally from Buffalo, New York, has roots in Barbados and Panama. Considering his father's Black Latino roots, many Afro-Latinos/as in DC see Mr. Fenty as a member of their community. Currently, Henry Jiménez is the Program Manager of DC's Department of Employment Services and the Deputy Director for Facilities Management, Donny Gonzalez, are both Afro-Latinos who hold leadership positions in Washington, DC's government. In addition, Julio Guity-Guevara, the former Deputy Director of the Mayor's Office on Latino Affairs (MOLA), recently held a prestigious post in the local government too. In 2000, Afro-Latino Arturo Griffiths was the Green Party Candidate for City Council At-Large in Washington, DC. His hopes to be the first self-identified Afro-Latino as an elected official was unsuccessful, and no other Afro-Latinos/as ran for a public seat. In other high leadership positions, Dr. Amanda Alexander, an Afro-Latina, currently serves as the Interim Chancellor for the District of Columbia Public Schools.

PURPOSE OF THE STUDY

Unlike the United States, Racial Democracy refers to certain patterns of race relations in Brazil. Specifically, it suggests that Brazilian race relations have developed in a tolerant and conflict-free manner, in contrast to the presumed hostile form of race relations that evolved in the United States. According to Antonio Sergio Guimaraes, a professor at the University of Sao Paulo, the usage goes back to the 1940s when the Brazilian anthropologist Arthur Ramos and French sociologist Roger Bastide (Encyclopedia of African-American Culture and History, 2006) employed the term Racial Democracy to link this pattern of race relations to Brazil's post-war democracy, which began to emerge at the end of the dictatorship of Getulio Vargas (1937–1945). However, the concept is more generally associated with the work of Gilberto Freyre (1900–1987), who proposed the idea in the 1930s in a departure from the scientific racist thinking that had prevailed within Brazilian intellectual circles since the beginning of the 20th Century (*Encyclopedia of African American Culture and History*, 2006).

Racial Democracy which serves as the basis for the theoretical framework for this book, represents a false narrative of racial equality in the Latino community. Furthermore, pigmentocracy is a discriminatory practice based on skin color and is a form of prejudice or discrimination in which human beings are treated differently based on the social meanings attached to skin color (Brennan, 2002) and continues to thrive and hamper the electability for Black Latinos/as to get gain access to political offices in Washington, DC. This book therefore seeks to contribute to the field of Political Science by examining the perspectives of Afro-Latinos/as to identify how ethnicity and colorism impacts their ability to be elected into political office. Also, this study questioned the discourse of Racial Democracy by examining the assumed concept of racial harmony in the Latino community by comparing the number of self-identified Afro-Latino/a residents in DC to the ethnicity of elected officials who represent them. This book further discussed if Racial Democracy in the Latino/a community in Washington, DC ensures equality for dark-skin self-identified Afro-Latino/as as it relates to their accessibility of becoming an elected official in the District of Columbia. I contend that more unity among the Afro-descendants of Latin heritage along with a stronger voter turnout within the Latino community may enhance Afro-Latinos/Latinas' electability in gaining more access to political offices in DC.

This book therefore seeks to shed light on the possible social/racial reasons that more Afro-Latinos/as have not been elected into public office in Washington, DC. Also, this project examined ethnic identity, the impact of skin-color plays on the well-being of Black Latinos/as and the low political representation of Afro-Latinos/as and the implications for the Black-Latino community in DC. Ultimately, the goal of this book is to identify the characterization of Afro-Latino/a identity in DC as well as to show the correlation between ethnicity and skin-color and how social/racial factors impact the electability of self-identified Afro-Latinos/as into political offices in Washington, DC. Furthermore, this work attempts to demonstrate that the lack of support from other Latino/a representatives helps contribute to low numbers of Latinos/as of African descent in political offices in the District of Columbia.

PROBLEM STATEMENT

The low political representation from the Afro-Latino/a community in political office in the District of Columbia is one that is problematic for political power of the community in particular as well as for the entire District of

Columbia. In general, as the Afro-Latino/a population continues to increase in Washington, DC as well as the United States, it is important that officials in political office reflect the people they represent. For the political power of the Afro-Latino community, low political representation means that the social/racial and economic needs of this community will continue to be unmet. For the District of Columbia, a jurisdiction of the United States in which its constituents are not represented in Congress in the same manner as citizens from the 50 states, low political representation means that members will have even less of a voice in the political arena.. The marginalization of political power of a minority group due to low Afro-Latino/a representation limits its ability to enjoy the full privileges of citizenship in the United States. Thus, this study proposed to investigate internal and external social/racial factors within the Afro-Latino community in order to offer remedies for this problem. The focus on these matters will allow me to contribute to the academic discourse and provide empirical evidence to ensure that knowledge is explored, questioned, exposed, and circulated.

MAJOR RESEARCH QUESTIONS

This project analyzed complex relationships between ethnicity, pigmentocracy, and political representation in the Black Latino community. Specifically, this work sought answers to the following two major research questions:

1. What social/racial factors influence the electability of light-skin and dark-skin self-identified Afro-Latinos/as running for political office in Washington, DC?
2. How do social/racial factors influence the pathway to political office for self-identified Afro-Latinos/as?

The study used a two-pronged approach to examine these questions. First, the internal and external social and political factors affecting the electability of Afro-Latinos/as to political office were investigated.

I proposed colorism as an internal factor shaping self-identity and ethnicity within the Afro-Latino/a community. I also proposed historical roots in colonialism, and racial structural issues in the US as external factors influencing the electability of Afro-Latinos/as into political office.

Regarding internal factors, I proposed that many Afro-Latinos/as in the US live out their existence through a "double-consciousness," a term coined by W. E. B. Du Bois to describe the internal conflict experienced by subordinated groups in an oppressive society. It is through this "double consciousness" that many Afro-Latinos/as try to prove to their Latino/a communities that they are both Black and Latino/a and that they navigate their own social and political positions as well as their interactions with other ethnic/racial groups and political systems in the United States. Regarding external factors, the study examined within the historical scenarios in which Latin American colonial political systems have favored citizens of European ancestry. As a result, many African descendants were considered inferior due in part to their Black, dark skin and/or African features. For the second part of my two-pronged approach, the study investigated the interplay between internal and external factors that are shaping the electability and influence of Afro-Latinos/as for political office. The standpoint consisted of the following arguments. First, I argued that a large majority of the Latino/a population of African descent vote on the grounds of "nationality" instead of "ethnicity" in Washington, DC. Second, I posited that Black Latinos/as of lighter complexions have a greater chance of getting into political office than their counterparts of darker hues.

HYPOTHESES

Based on the proceeding research questions vis-à-vis the social/racial factors that influence Afro-Latinos/as' electability into political office, the following hypotheses were suggested for empirical testing:

H1: Social/racial factors such as ethnicity and pigmentocracy influence the electability of light-skin and dark-skin self-identified Afro-Latino/as running for political office in Washington, DC.

H2: Social/racial factors influence the pathway to political office for self-identified Afro-Latinos/as in Washington, DC.

First, in probing, analyzing, and explaining the contributing factors that underlie why self-identified Afro-Latinos/as have not been elected into political offices in DC at least in the last decade, the research proposed that it is due to a lack of support from the non-Afro-Latino/a voters. The cultural and social/racial persuasions which make many Latinos/as of African descent choose their nationality over their ethnicity could greatly impact the election process, and/or appointments of Afro-Latinos/as to political offices. While more social visibilities in the arts, literature, and social media have begun to increase for Afro-Latinos/as, their political representation remains a stagnant challenge. Second, the research proposed that Racial Democracy Theory has birthed a false narrative of social/racial equality within the Latino community and that this sense of equality has limited Black, dark-skin, and/or Afro-Latinos/as from eligibility and electability to political office. Therefore, it is postulated that pigmentocracy plays a significant role in determining which ethnicity in the Latino community gains access to political office.

METHODOLOGY

In this section, the research methodology employed in the study is explicated. Primarily, the research is qualitative, as I employed an interpretive and naturalistic approach which examined the subject matter. Qualitative research is primarily exploratory research. This type of research in methodology was best used to gain an understanding of underlying reasons, opinions, and motivations. Also, it provided insights into the problems and helped to develop ideas or hypotheses for potential quantitative research. In addition, qualitative research was also used to uncover trends in thought and opinions, and dive deeper into the problem.

A combination of the Descriptive and the Explanator Case Study method was utilized for this study. The Descriptive Case Study method helped me to describe the characteristics of the population. The Explanatory Case Study method was used to focus primarily on describing the nature of the demographic segment, while emphasizing the why factor. A case study, while narrow in scope, provided an opportunity to fully understand the dynamics operating in Washington, DC in terms of Afro-Latinos/as pursuing and achieving political office. The conceptual and theoretical frameworks that undergird this qualitative study are discussed in the following two sections.

CONCEPTUAL FRAMEWORK

The discourse on colorism as it impacts the ability of Afro-Latinos/as to achieve political office hinges upon three principal attributes:

1. the characterization of being Afro-Latino/a (CBAL) in the United States, specifically in DC;
2. the politics of ethnicity versus nationalism (PEVN); and
3. pigmentocracy's impact on the opportunity and electability of Latinos/as of African descent (PIOELAD) in political offices in Washington, DC.

As defined earlier, CBAL in the United States refers to the distinctive description of a Black Hispanic or Afro-Hispanic (Spanish:Afrohispano) who is racially Black and is from Latin America and/or speaks the Spanish language natively; PEVN refers to the fact or state of belonging to a social group that has a common national or cultural tradition and the exclusion and inclusion of a group just as racism does; and PIOELAD connotes a discriminatory practice based on skin color and is a form of prejudice or discrimination in which human beings are treated differently based on the social meanings attached to skin color. The connections among these attributes are diagrammatically represented in Figure 0.1.

As can be noted in Figure 0.1, CBAL, PEVN, and PIOELAD are suggested to jointly influence the ability of Afro-Latinos/as to achieve political office. The framework represents a continuing sequence of attributes in a circular flow. Each attribute has the same level of importance; hence, sequential directions are not indicated. The framework is therefore conceptual in that as Chava Frankfort Nachmias and David Nachmias point out, in a conceptual framework, which constitutes "the third level of theory, descriptive categories are systematically placed in a broad structure of explicit propositions, statements of relationships between two or more empirical properties, to be accepted or rejected" (Frankfort-Nachmias and Nachmias, 1996, p. 38).

THEORETICAL FRAMEWORK

As stated earlier, the philosophical model that served as the theoretical framework for this study is Racial Democracy Theory, which generally refers to certain patterns of race relations within a system of government by the whole population or all the eligible members of a state, typically through elected representatives. Specifically, it suggests that in the case of Brazil, race relations have developed in a tolerant and conflict-free manner, in contrast to the hostile form of race relations that evolved in the United States. According to Antonio Sergio Guimaraes, a professor at the University of Sao Paulo, the usage of Racial Democracy Theory goes back to the 1940s, when the

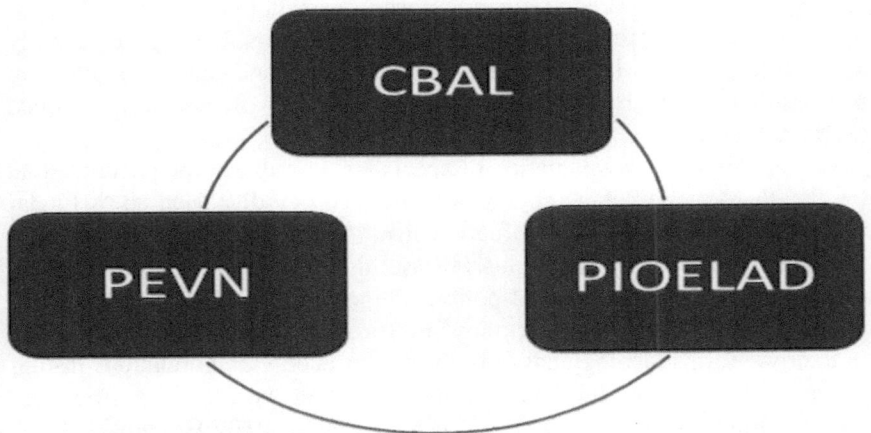

Figure 0.1: Conceptual Framework of the Ability for Afro-Latinos/as to Achieve Public Office. Source: Self-generated by Author.

Brazilian anthropologist Arthur Ramos and French sociologist Roger Bastide employed the term to link this pattern of race relations to Brazil's post war democracy, which began to emerge at the end of the dictatorship of Getulio Vargas (1937–1945) (Encyclopedia.com, 2019, p. 1). Nonetheless, the theory is more generally associated with the work of Gilberto Freyre (1900–1987), who proposed the idea in the 1930s in a departure from the scientific racist thinking that had prevailed within Brazilian intellectual circles since the beginning of the 20th Century (Encyclopedia of African American Culture and History, 2006).

In 1965, sociologist Florestan Fernandes defined the notion of racial democracy as a "myth." For him, it is a synonym for "ideology" in the sense of "false consciousness." Fernandes and his associates were essentially concerned that the celebration of racial tolerance in Brazil camouflaged the actual socioeconomic exclusion of Blacks, since they were unqualified to get jobs in the emerging industrial sector. Fernandes along with Thales de Azevedo, René Ribeiro and Luiz de Aguiar Costa Pinto, Charley Wagley, Roger Bastide and Alfred Métraux, collected and analyzed data in cities such as Rio de Janeiro, Recife, São Paulo, and Salvador. In general, these studies showed that Brazilian racial democracy was a myth and that non-White people experienced racism in the job market and encountered difficulties in climbing the socioeconomic ladder (Serrao, 2019). Based on UNESCO's published findings, several other empirical studies concluded that racial democracy was, in fact, an ideology that included racism and made it more difficult for Black and Brown Brazilians to close opportunity gaps with the White population (Maio, 1997).

For historian and anthropologist Lilia Schwarcz, "racial democracy" was entirely discredited when the Black activist movement fighting for real equality and inclusion denounced the perils of following its ideology. By simply refusing to contend with racial inequalities, political and economic elites can rest assured that their roles in perpetuating racism will not be questioned (Serrao, 2019).

In the 1970s, a new generation of specialists introduced the postulate that the "myth of racial democracy" is a racist ideology disguised as "a fundamental component of Brazilian nationalism (Marx, 1997). Despite creating the appearance of unity and inclusiveness, this ideology was in fact a crucial element of an "unofficial racial policy," forged by the elites and backed by the State, to assure "White hegemony" in Brazilian society (Hanchard, 1994). In their view, this ideology has only fostered peaceful racial relations insofar it has masked White elites' racism and concealed the association between race and life changes (for example, see Nascimento, 1978; Hasenbalg, 1978; Skidmore, 1993; Winant, 1994; Burdick, 1992; Brown, 1997; Twine, 2001).

Also, in the past four decades, beginning around the publication in 1974 of Thomas E. Skidmore's Black into White, a revisionist study of Brazilian race relations, scholars began to criticize the notion that Brazil is actually a "racial democracy." Skidmore (1992) argues that the predominantly White elite within Brazilian society promoted racial democracy to obscure very real forms of racial oppression.

Michael Hanchard (1994), a political scientist at Johns Hopkins University, has argued that the ideology of racial democracy, often promoted by state apparatuses, prevents effective action to combat racial discrimination by leading people to ascribe discrimination to other forms of oppression and allowing government officials charged with preventing racism to deny its existence. Also, France Winddance Twine's 1997 ethnography appears to support these contentions.

Lastly Hanchard (1994) has compiled findings from a great deal of research conducted by other scholars demonstrating widespread discrimination in employment, education, and electoral politics. The seemingly paradoxical use of racial democracy to obscure the realities of racism has been referred to by Florestan Fernandes (1969) as the "prejudice of having no prejudices." That is, because the state assumes the absence of racial prejudice, it fails to enforce what few laws exist to counter racial discrimination, as it believes that such efforts are unnecessary.

DATA COLLECTION AND SAMPLING TECHNIQUES

The objective of the study examined the proposed impact ethnicity and pigmentocracy has on the electability among Black and darker Latinos/as into political office in Washington, DC. As such, this study addresses the following questions: (1) What social/racial factors influence the electability of light-skin and dark-skin self-identified Afro-Latinos/as running for political office in Washington, DC? (2) How do social/racial factors influence the pathway to political office for self-identified Afro-Latinos/as? To answer these questions, I used structured interviews which generated qualitative data using closed-ended questions. This form of questioning allowed me to develop a real sense of the interviewees' understanding of my project. My methodology consisted of two components. The first component entailed in-depth interviews and the second included a descriptive explanatory case study.

Using a snowball sampling technique, I interviewed at least ten U.S. citizens who currently live in the Washington, DC metro area, with lineages from Dominican Republic or Central and South America. The subjects were of voting age (age 18) and eligible to vote.

DATA SOURCES

The interview protocol adapted from protocols utilized by Reuel Rogers (2006) and Jackson, Hutchings, Brown and Wong (2004), and focused on three key themes: (1) ethnicity/identity, (2) pigmentocracy, and (3) political representation. The In-depth Interviews included (a) background and context (b), identity (c), political interest, and (d) pigmentocracy (see Table 3.1 Interview Participants). The interviewees were self-identified Afro-Latinos/as living in Washington, DC. The interviews were conducted on a population of males and females between the ages of 18 and 75 years of age. The selection of interviewees ranged in terms of social economic backgrounds and the interviews were voluntary.

DATA ANALYTICAL TECHNIQUES

In order to determine if skin color impacts the electability of Afro-Latinos/as in Washington, DC, I utilized a qualitative approach. For the qualitative analysis, content analysis was used in this study. This technique is defined by Frankfort, Nachmias, and DeWaard et al. as "any technique for making inferences by systematically and objectively identifying specified characteristics of messages" (Frankfort, Nachmias, and DeWaard, 2014, p. 31). As noted by Bangura and Hopwood (2014), the method of content analysis is extremely essential for teasing out the subtleties of different styles of communication among scholarly texts in addition to media reports, speeches by politicians, letters, Supreme Court opinions, as well as discord with regards to composition and authorship of a certain book.

Content analysis thus, as expressed by Bangura, Thomas, and Hopwood, contains five categories that constitute its various forms: (1) words or terms, (2) themes, (3) characters, (4) paragraphs, and (5) items (Bangura, Thomas, and Hopwood, 2014). The reality is that the researcher is obligated to decide which unit of analysis to use, and this choice will depend both on practical considerations and the nature of the research questions. Once decided, the researcher can expect some form of quantification to be added in the analysis. This can happen in three various ways: (1) frequency of a certain word or term, (2) measurement of intensity regarding particular words used, and (3) a calculation of space of placement of certain word within a text. Each of these designs can be used to check critical information concerning communicators' aims and meanings of particular messages (Bangura, Thomas, and Hopwood, 2014).

ORGANIZATION OF THE REST OF THE BOOK

Chapter 1 discusses the theoretical framework and research methodology. The philosophical model that serves as the theoretical framework for this research is Racial Democracy Theory, which generally refers to certain patterns of race relations within a system of government by the whole population or all the eligible members of a state, typically through elected representatives.

In this introduction, the research methodology employed in the study is explained. Primarily, the research was qualitative, as I employ an interpretive and naturalistic approach to examine the subject matter. Qualitative research is primarily exploratory research. This type of research methodology was best used to gain an understanding of underlying reasons, opinions, and motivations. Also, it provides insights into the problem and helped me to develop ideas for potential quantitative research.

A combination of the Descriptive and the Explanator Case Study methods was used to analyze the data collected in this study. A case study, while narrow in scope, provided an opportunity to fully understand the dynamics operating in Washington, DC in terms of Afro-Latinos/as pursuing and achieving public office. For this study, both primary and secondary data is utilized for this research. Primary data was collected from self-identified Afro-Latino/a interviewees. Secondary data was retrieved from books, journals, magazines, newspapers, and reliable online sources on the subject.

Chapter 1 discusses the term *pigmentocracy* as well as provides an overview of the ethnicities of Latin America. In this chapter, historical content regarding ethnic compositions in Washington, DC as well as the Latino/a community will be provided to the reader. Also, this chapter provides background on Washington, DC and the Afro-Latino/a political officials. In addition, there will be a discussion on colorism in the Afro-Latino/a community.

Chapter 2 entails a review of the competing perspectives that pertained to the topic under investigation and comprised of journal articles and books that captures the nexus among Black self-identity, pigmentocracy, and political representation. This chapter examines the works of scholars in relation to the electability of dark-skin self-identified Afro-Latinos/as into political office and explores concepts such as formalistic representation, symbolic representation, substantive representation and descriptive representation, and how these notions apply in the case of the Afro-Latino/a voting community.

There is a brief theoretical discussion on identity and the competing perspectives are organized in a synchronic approach based on the three themes from the conceptual framework: (1) Afro-Latino/a Identity in the Americas and the United States; (2) Views Regarding Ethnicity and Pigmentocracy in the Latino Community; and (3) Descriptive Representation and Electability of Dark-skin Self-identified Afro-Latinos/as to Political Office. Also, there is a discussion that covered the limitations in the competing perspectives.

Chapter 3 deals with the first major research question of the study. To restate the question: What social/racial factors influence the electability of light-skin and dark-skin self-identified Afro-Latinos/as running for political office in Washington, DC? This chapter is divided into three sections. The first section provides a conceptual discussion on ethnicity; the second section presents the qualitative results; the third section analyzes the findings and determines the validity of the hypothesis of the major research question investigated in this chapter.

Chapter 4 deals with the second major research question of the study: How do social/racial factors influence the pathway to political office for self-identified Afro-Latinos/as in Washington, DC? This chapter is divided into four sections. The first section provides a theoretical discussion on representing and theories of representation; the second section provides a theoretical discussion on typology or representation; the third section entails a discussion of the qualitative results; the fourth section analyzes and determines the validity of the hypothesis of the major research question probed in this chapter. This chapter also evaluated the pathway to political office for self-identified Afro-Latinos/as in Washington, DC.

Chapter 5 is divided into three sections. The first section provides the summary of the research; section two discusses the conclusions; section three offers policy recommendations.

Chapter 1

Background

In this chapter, I provide a discussion on the term *pigmentocracy* and give a general overview of the many ethnicities in Latin America. This chapter covers data regarding the ethnic compositions in Washington, DC as well as in the Latino/a community. Also, this chapter will provides empirical data on Latino/a elected officials and political officials in the U.S. and more specially amongst the Afro-Latino/a community. Lastly, this chapter provides a discussion on colorism in the Afro-Latino/a community.

PIGMENTOCRACY

In the past couple of decades, the word *pigmentocracy* has come into common usage to refer to the distinctions that people of African descent in America make in their various skin tones, which can range from the darkest shades of black to paleness that approximates whiteness. Moreover, the "ocracy" in pigmentocracy carries with its notions of hierarchical value that observers place on such skin tones. Therefore, lighter skin tones are valued more than darker skin tones.

In 1944, Alejandro Lipschutz, a Chilean anthropologist, coined the term pigmentocracy to refer to the ethnic and color-based hierarchies of Latin America. In his text, Lipschutz referred to pigmentocracy sometimes as a hierarchy based on a color continuum and other times as an ethnoracial hierarchy with whites on top, indigenous and black people at the bottom and mestizos in the middle, thus glossing over differences between the two classification systems.

Oxford dictionary defines *pigmentocracy* as "a system of social or class distinction based on skin colour; a society based on such a system; the dominant group in such a society." While Etymology dictionary defines *pigmentocracy* as "a social or governmental hierarchy based on skin tone regardless of race," usually in a South African context, apparently coined in "The Economist," from pigment +-cracy "rule or government by."

As such, these preferences have social, economic, and political implications, as persons of lighter skin tones historically were frequently—and stereotypically—viewed as being more intelligent and socially acceptable than their darker skinned black counterparts. Also, darker black people were viewed as unattractive and generally considered of lesser value. In addition, Europeans standards of beauty dominated much of Latin America for centuries. Although the word *pigmentocracy* may have come into widespread usage fairly recently, the concept extends throughout the history of Latin America.

During slavery, black people who were fathered by their white masters often gained privileges based on their lighter coloring. One reported pattern is that blacks of lighter skin color were reputedly selected to work in the Big Houses of plantation masters while blacks of darker hues were routinely sent to the fields, (Harris, 2022). Moreover, one of the origins of the Dozens, the ritual game of insult in African American culture, is reputed to have developed as a result of slurs darker skinned blacks who worked in the fields hurled at lighter skinned blacks because their mothers had given birth to children sired by white masters. Some masters who recognized their paternity publicly sometimes sent their partially colored offspring to the North to be educated. According to Harris, this practice explains in part the belief that blacks of lighter skin were more intelligent and had more educational opportunities.

It was convenient to the mythology of slavery to suggest this pattern as well, for even without formal admission, whites were aware that some blacks looked more like them than others. Harris argues that since many theories of bestiality and dehumanization were aligned with darker skinned blacks, it was perhaps preferable to be more tolerant of the lighter skinned black people. However, it was a consistent pattern, for theories also developed about mongrelization, that is, the mixing of black and white blood, leading to extreme anti-social behavior in persons so endowed. Value based on skin tones led to some interesting historical developments both within and outside the black communities. To prevent blacks fathered by white masters from making claims on their masters, children born to enslaved women were legally designated to take the status of those women. Therefore, blond-haired, blue-eyed enslaved persons could not change their condition through any legal process. Also, to ensure that this pattern could not be broken, anyone determined to have had black blood in one of their ancestors five generations removed was still designated "Negro." That meant that mulattoes, quadroons, octoroons, sextaroons, and any person who had 1/32 black blood were all designated to be fully black by laws of American society. "The mighty drop" of black blood, as some scholars refer to it, was powerful enough to control generations of persons legally classified as black who might otherwise have been classed as white or who might have passed for white.

Many persons who skin complexion was light enough to pass for white, did indeed do so. With their straight hair and Europeans features, they simply left their "black" identities behind, moved into white society, and became "white." Some blacks made this move for financial reasons and continued to return to black communities to remain connected. While others assumed completely new identities and did not look back.

As Harris argues, politics surrounded both decisions. Given the climate of the late nineteenth century, when any educated person of African descent was expected to use his or her education to help other blacks, to depart completely for the white world was considered a form of abandonment as well as a form of racial self-hatred. Nonetheless, many persons did take advantage of this biological option, while others remained committed to their fellow blacks and used their advantages of skin color and education to help them.

ETHNICITIES OF LATIN AMERICA

In this section, I will cover a brief history of the origins of the terms associated with Afro-Latino/a, and Afro-Latin American. Also, I will provide a general overview of the ethnicities that define persons of Latin American descent.

In the United States, the identity of people of African descent from Latin America has changed over time. Authors such as Juan Flores and Miriam Jiménez Román argue that Afro-Latinos/as, are described as "people of African descent in Mexico, Central and South America, and the Spanish-speaking Caribbean and by extension those of African descent in the United States whose origins are in Latin America and the Caribbean." This section explores the history, terminology and definitions of Latinos and more specifically Afro–Latin Americans, Black Latin Americans, Black Latino Americans.

The term Afro–Latin American is not widely used in Latin America outside academic circles and usually Afro–Latin Americans are called Black Latin Americans of African ancestry and may also be denoted by the prefix Afro-plus a specific nationality, such as Afro-Brazilian, Afro-Cuban or Afro-Haitian (wiki/Afro-Latin_Americans). In addition, Black Latino Americans, also called Afro-Latinos or Black Latinos, are classified by the United States Census Bureau, Office of Management and Budget and other United States government agencies as black people living in the United States with ancestry in Latin America and/or who speak Spanish or Portuguese as their first language. Moreover, Afro-Latin or Black Latin Americans are Latin Americans of full or mainly African ancestry.

Between 1502 and 1866, 11.2 million Africans disembarked from slave ships in the New World during the Middle Passage. And out of the 11.2 million people, only 450,000 came to the United States. The rest of the African slaves who survived on the Middle Passage were taken to the Caribbean, Latin America and South America (Gates 2011.) According to Gates, the descendants of slaves brought to Latin America don't identify as white or black the way many Americans do. He states for instance, in Brazil there are 134 categories of blackness to describe someone of African descent. Therefore, understanding the many ethnicities in the Latin America will help understand the complexity of identity among Latinos/Latinas as well as provide context in explaining why identifying as Afro-Latino/a isn't based on physical appearance only.

To begin, the indigenous population of Latin America, the Amerindians, arrived during the Lithic stage. The Lithic stage was the earliest period of human occupation in the Americas, as post-glacial hunter gatherers spread through the Americas. In post-Columbian times they experienced tremendous population decrease, particularly in the early decades of colonization. They have since recovered in numbers, surpassing sixty million by some estimates. With the growth of other ethnicities, the Amerindians now compose a majority only in Bolivia and Guatemala, and nearly a half of Peru's population. Besides the aforementioned countries, Mexico has the largest Amerindian population in the Americas in total numbers, ranging roughly one fifth of national population. Most of the remaining countries have Amerindian minorities, in every case making up less than one-tenth of the respective country's population. In many countries, people of mixed Amerindian and European ancestry make up the majority of the population.

People of Asian descent make up several million in Latin America. The first Asians to settle in the Latin America were Filipino due to Spain's trading in Asia and the Americas. The majority of Asian Latin Americans are of Japanese or Chinese ancestry and reside mainly in Brazil and Peru. Also, there is a growing Chinese minority in Panama. The country of Brazil is home to about two million people of Asian descent which includes the largest ethnic Japanese community outside Japan itself (estimated as high as 1.5 million), and about 200,000 ethnic Chinese and 100,000 ethnic Koreans. Also, ethnic Koreans number tens of thousands in countries such as Argentina and Mexico. The country of Peru with 1.47 million people of Asian descent, has one of the largest Chinese communities in the world, with nearly one million Peruvians being of Chinese ancestry. There is a strong ethnic-Japanese presence in Peru, where a past president and several politicians are of Japanese descent.

Beginning in the late 15th century, large numbers of Iberian colonists settled in what became Latin America. The Portuguese primarily colonized Brazil and the Spaniards settled throughout the region. Currently, most White

Latin Americans are of Spanish, Portuguese and Italian ancestry. Iberians brought the Spanish and Portuguese languages, the Catholic faith, and many Iberian-Latin traditions. Countries such as Brazil, Argentina, Mexico, Chile, Colombia and Venezuela contain the largest numbers of Whites in Latin America. Self-identified populations of whites make up the majorities in countries such as Argentina, Chile, Costa Rica, and Uruguay, and nearly half of Brazil's and Venezuela's population, Lizcano (2005).

Since most of Latin America gained independence in the 1810s–1820s, millions of people have immigrated there. According to the Britannica Online Encyclopedia, of these immigrants, Italians formed the largest group, and next were Spaniards and Portuguese. Many other European immigrants arrived, such as the French, Germans, Greeks, Poles, Ukrainians, Russians, Croats, Estonians, Latvians, Lithuanians, Irish, and Welsh. Also, people from the Middle East such as Jews and Arabs of Lebanese, Syrian, and Palestinian descent migrated to Latin America. Whites presently compose the largest racial group in Latin America and, whether as White, Mestizo, or Mulatto, the vast majority of Latin Americans have white ancestry.

Lastly, as mentioned earlier in this section, millions of Africans were brought to Latin America from the 16th century onward. The majority of Africans were shipped as slaves and sent to the Caribbean region and Latin America. Currently, Brazil leads this category in complete numbers among the Latin American countries, with 39% of the population being of at least partial Afro-Latin American descent. Other countries with populations with significant sizes of Black Latinos/as are found in Dominican Republic, Puerto Rico, Colombia, Cuba, Panama, Ecuador, Peru, Venezuela, Honduras, and Costa Rica. Latin Americans of mixed Black and White ancestry, called Mulattoes, are more numerous than Blacks. However, sometimes mulattos are included in the 'black' category, while other times they form their own ethnicity.

The intermixing between Europeans and Amerindians began early in the colonial period and was extensive. As a result, people known as Mestizos (Caboclos in Brazil), make up the majority of the population in half of the countries of Latin America, making Paraguay one of the leading countries. Additionally, Mestizos compose large minorities in nearly all the other mainland countries. While Mulattoes are people of mixed African and European ancestry.

In Latin America, Mulattoes descend primarily from Spanish or Portuguese men and enslaved African women. In the country of Brazil, mulattoes make up Latin America's largest population. In addition, Mulattoes are a population majority in the Dominican Republic as well as Cuba. Also, Mulattoes make up large numbers in countries such as Venezuela, Panama, Honduras, Colombia, and Costa Rica. Similarly, smaller populations of mulattoes are found in other Latin American countries such as Peru, Ecuador, Uruguay, Nicaragua, Paraguay, Bolivia and Mexico.

Lastly, Zambos, the intermixing between Africans and Amerindians was very prevalent in Brazil and Central America, often due to slaves running away (becoming cimarrones: maroons) and being taken in by Amerindian villagers. In Spanish speaking countries, people of this mixed ancestry are known as Zambos, Garifunas in Central America, Lobos in Mexico, and Cafuzos in Brazil.

During the colonial period, the Spaniards dominated Latin America and began using indigenous laborers to exploit the natural resources of the "new world," which was rich in precious metals and agricultural lands (Casaus Arzu, 2009; Tanck de Estrada & Marichal, 2010). Nevertheless, as the percentage of the indigenous population declined, the Spaniards found themselves in need of additional laborers. Such need gave rise to the slave trade and more than 10 million African slaves were brought to Latin America. Therefore, understanding the historical makeup of Latin America sheds light on the complexity of identifying an Afro-Latino/a in the United States and how skin-color complicates social, economic, and political matters in the Latino community.

WASHINGTON, DC AND THE LATINO/A COMMUNITY

Indeed, the District of Columbia is known for its many historical memorials that include the Washington Monument, Lincoln Memorial, Korean War Veterans Memorial, and the Martin Luther King, Jr. Memorial. The vastness of the number of monuments in the District is only one great aspect of Washington, DC. The other great facet of this city is its rich diversity of communities, which makes DC one of the most diverse cities in the United States (*The Washington Post*, September 6, 2012). Historically, DC has been a city with a largely African American population, becoming a majority Black city in the 1950s–1960s. However, the number of Blacks declined during the last two decades. Table 1.1 shows the current ethnic composition for the three

Table 1.1: Ethnic Composition in Washington, DC
Source: U.S. Census Bureau, (2017)

Race	[Year] Population
Black	49.0%
White	43.6%
Asian	2.0%
Hispanic	4.0%
Other	1.4%

largest ethnic groups in Washington, DC. The city's make-up is 49 percent Black, 43.6 percent White, 2.0 percent Asian, 4.0 percent for Hispanic and 1.4 percent Other.

When it comes to the civic engagement at the local, national and international levels, Washington, DC is a vibrant city of collaboration. Lawmakers, lobbyists, political activists, students and intellectuals collaborate and meet to debate major issues, legislation, and public policies within the political arena. In addition, diplomats, other foreign dignitaries, and international government officials come to Washington, DC to meet with domestic government officials to express and represent the interests of their countries and citizens. But who are the political representatives who advocate on behalf of the various communities in DC? According to the US Census Bureau's national population totals from 2010 to 2017, Washington, DC surpasses the populations of some states such as Vermont and Wyoming. In addition, Washington, DC is ranked number one by population density (i.e., the number of people per square mile of land area) compared to a large state such as New Jersey (ipl.org). However, the District of Columbia is not one of the 50 states. Due to this situation, Washington, DC has no Senators in the U.S. Senate or Representatives in the U.S. House. Its one member in the House of Representatives, an office held by Eleanor Norton (Democrat, At-Large), is only a delegate with limited voting privileges. Delegates from districts have marginalized roles in Congress and their constituents are not represented in the same manner as most citizens in the 50 states.

In 2018, Washington, DC elected a Black mayor, Muriel Bowser, along with 13 members to the DC Council. The Council consisted of seven White members and six Black members. However, while DC has a considerably large Latino/a community, none of these elected officials on the Council are Hispanic/Latino/a. According to the US Census Bureau's Census 2000 data for the District of Columbia, Washington, DC boasted 572,059 residents that year. Hispanic or Latino/a (of any race) made up 44,953 or 7.9 percent of that population. Of the Hispanic community, Mexicans made up 5,098 or 0.9 percent; Puerto Ricans made up 2,328 or 0.4 percent; and Cubans made up 1,101 or 0.2 percent, while "Other Hispanic or Latino/a (of any race)" made up 41,324 or 6.4 percent of the population. Figure 1.1 illustrates the Hispanic racial demographics in Washington, DC in 2000; Figure 1.2 illustrates the Hispanic racial demographics in Washington, DC in 2010.

Furthermore, according to the U.S. Census Bureau's 2010 Census, the total population of residents living in the District of Columbia was 601,723 with Whites making up 231,471 or 38.5 percent, Blacks or African Americans 305,125 or 50.7 percent and Hispanic or Latinos/as (of any race) 54,749 or 9.1 percent.

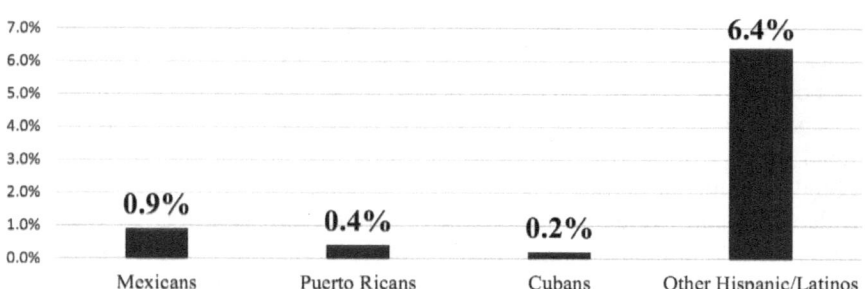

Figure 1.1: Hispanic Racial Demographics in Washington, DC. Source: US Census Bureau (2000).

Within the Hispanic or Latino/a demographics in DC, Mexicans made up 8,507 or 8 percent; Puerto Ricans 3,129 or 0.5; Cubans 1,789 or 0.3 percent; and Dominicans (Dominican Republic) 2,508 or 0.4 percent of the population. Also, in the Hispanic or Latino/a and race section, Latinos/as self-identified as White alone are 22,007 or 3.7 percent; Black or African American alone are 4,072 or 0.7 percent; Asian alone are 238 or 0.0 percent; Some Other race alone are 22,923 or 3.8; and Two or More races are 4,666 or 0.8 percent (US Census Bureau, 2010).

In July of 2016, the U.S. Census Bureau estimated DC's population to be 604,453. Estimates showed the Hispanic or Latino/a percentage was 10.9 percent of the total population. Census statistics, oral histories, archival and secondary sources indicate that the Hispanic or Latino community originated with Mexican Americans, Puerto Ricans, Cubans, and Dominicans in the mid-20th Century when they migrated from the Southern Cone in the 1970s. Bolivians, Peruvians, Salvadorans, and more Mexicans followed during in the 1990s and have continued to settle in the nation's capital ever since (Metropolitan Policy Program, 2010).

Historically, Hispanics and Latinos/as in Washington, DC have lived in the northwest quadrant of the city, primarily in Wards 1 and 2. However, in recent years, changes in the city's neighborhoods and housing market have resulted in a shift in the areas where Latinos/as live. The District's housing boom, which started in 2001 and peaked in 2006, affected Latino/a neighborhoods. Most recently, the Latino/a population has increased in Ward 4 along its southern border and declined in Wards 2 and 3. The District's Latino community has predominantly lived in Columbia Heights, Park View, and Mt. Pleasant in Ward 1, and more recently in Brightwood Park, Crestwood, and Petworth in Ward 4 (The Urban Institute, 2009, p. 18). While there is a larger presence of Latinos/as in these neighborhoods, there is still no Latino/a representation or specifically Afro-Latino/a that represents them in any public office (DC Board of Elections, 2016).

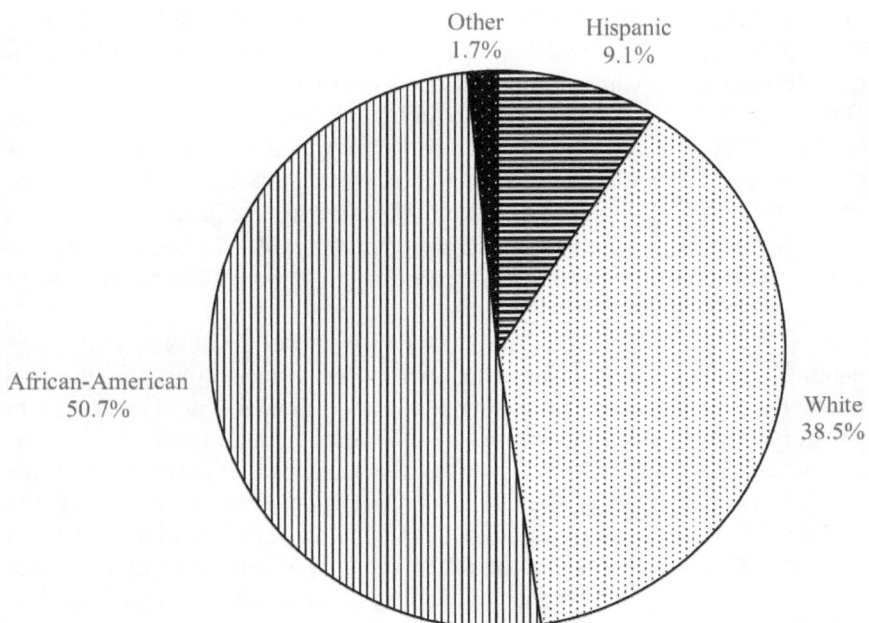

Figure 1.2: Racial Demographics in Washington, DC. Source: US Census Bureau (2000).

According to the U.S. Census Bureau's 2016 ACS 1-Year Survey on Race Data, 74,422 Hispanic or Latinos/as reside in Washington, DC. Out of this number, 4,706 consider themselves to be Black or African American. Overall, the Northeast region has the largest concentration of Black Latinos/as partly because of the large Puerto Rican, Dominican, and other mostly or partly African-descended Hispanic populations in the region. In comparison to DC, states along the East Coast like New York, Massachusetts, Pennsylvania, New Jersey, and Connecticut have some of the highest percentages of Hispanics identifying as Black (U.S. Census Bureau, 2003). In these states, up to 24 percent of Hispanics identify as Black, compared to 2.5 percent of Hispanics nationwide (U.S. Census Bureau, 2013).

WASHINGTON, DC AND AFRO-LATINO/A POLITICAL OFFICIALS

In early 2020, less than 10 percent of the U.S. House of Representatives were Latino/a, despite Latinos making up 18.5 percent of the population (https://salud-america.org). In 2018, 41 Latinos were elected to U.S. Congress, 33 Democrats and 6 Republicans (www.hispanicoutlook.com). According to the *List of Hispanic and Latino Americans in the United States Congress*, in 2017, there was only one self-identified Latino of African descent in a federal elected office, Adriano Espaillat (D-NY) (*New York Daily News*, 2017). During the 2020 election, one Latino and one Latina of African ancestry ran for the United States Congress. Ritchie Torres was the youngest member of the New York City Council elected to represent the Bronx. An Afro-Latino of Puerto Rican decent, he successfully defeated his challenger to represent New York's 15th Congressional District making Mr. Torres (D-NY) the second self-identified Latino of African descent to be elected to the United States Congress.

Also, Ms. Candance Valenzuela (D-TX) who ran an unsuccessful campaign for the 24th Congressional District in Texas stood to become the first Black Latina elected to U.S. Congress. In addition, if she was elected to Congress, she would have become just the third Latina elected from Texas (www.nbcnews.com). The low political representation of numbers from the Afro-Latino/a community stands out as a persistent pattern when compared to their White counterparts throughout the United States as well as in Latin America. Whether it was blatant exclusion or the semblance of inclusion, access to political offices in the U.S. has historically privileged Latinos/as of European descent.

COLORISM IN THE AFRO-LATINO/A COMMUNITY

During the 1970s and 1980s, whether by off-spring or migration, the visibility of Latinos/as of African descent began to grow across the United States, especially in places such as the South and Northeast regions (Gustavo Lopez and Ana Gonzalez-Barrera, 2016). While many Afro-Latinos/as migrated to the United States in search of social mobility and economic opportunities, many often found themselves in the crosshairs of the country's institutional discriminatory structures. Often racially stigmatized even within their own Latino/a communities, research shows that many Afro-Latinos/as identified as either Latino/a or Black American (Hernandez, 2003). And, according to the Pew Research Center Fact Tank (2019), about two-thirds of Hispanics with darker-skin color report they have experienced discrimination or been treated unfairly regularly or from time to time, compared with half of those with lighter-skin tones.

Often, the United States racial structure left many Black and darker Latinos/as with no other choice but to succumb to the demands of racial categorization. Some studies indicate that Black Latinos/as are more likely to have less education, lower incomes, less employment, and higher incarnation rates compared to their White counterparts (The Social Inequality Matrix in Latin America, 2016). In addition, many Black or darker-skin Latinos/as identify with their country of origin in order not to be categorized as African American or Black in the United States context. Other studies show that language, dress, social and/or professional association and even hairstyles are adopted by Black or dark-skin Latinos/as in order to differentiate themselves from African Americans (Austin and Middleton, 2015).

With the 21st Century election of the mostly identified first Black President of the United States, a wave of Black consciousness spread throughout the U.S. This was especially apparent among Afro-Latinos/as living in states such as New York and New Jersey (U.S. Census Bureau, 2013). Colorism, along with the biological misconceptions about persons of African descent created deception and perpetuated the narrative that dark-skin equals inferiority. As noted by *The Hill*, of the 38 Hispanic members across both chambers of Congress, 34 in the House and four members in the Senate only one, Adriano Espaillat (D-NY), self-identifies as a Latino of African descent (*The Hill*, 2017).

Tension within the rigid United States racial structure may cause many Afro-Latinos/as to choose a racial category which, in turn, may influence many of them to vote for a political candidate based on national identity while disregarding his/her ethnic identity. Also, the ideologies imposed upon Latin America due to its colonization by both Europe and the United States have engendered an ongoing process of self-identification and re-identification which continues well into the 21st Century (Garcés Montes, 2007). As the Afro-Latino/a population in the United States continues to grow more ethnically diverse, greater attention is required for establishing a representative social and political relationship.

Chapter 2

Competing Perspectives

Various observers writing about the topic under investigation have offered many competing perspectives on the connection among Black self-identity, pigmentocracy, and political representation. This chapter examines the points of views in relations to electability of dark-skin self-identified Afro-Latinos/as into political office and explores concepts such as formalistic representation, symbolic representation, substantive representation and descriptive representation and how these notions apply in the case of the Afro-Latino/a voting community.

The ensuring discussions is organized in a synchronic approach based on the three themes from the conceptual framework: (1) Afro-Latino/a identity in the Americas and the United States; (2) Views Regarding Ethnicity and Pigmentocracy in the Latino Community; and (3) Descriptive Representation and Electability of Dark-skin Self-identified Afro-Latinos/as to Political Office. The objective is to provide the reader a systematic perspective of the competing perspectives. But before doing all this, however, I will first provide a general conceptual discussion of the term *ethnicity* that undergirds the various facets of this book for those readers who may not be familiar with its theoretical complexities. This will serve as a backdrop for understanding the theoretical groundings in the sections that will follow.

ETHNICITY: A CONCEPTUAL DISCUSSION

The conceptualization of *ethnicity* has generally centered on the following three aspects: (1) competing definitions, (2) ethnicity as a social fact, and (3) the functionalist versus the conflict perspective on ethnicity. These aspects are discussed sequentially in the rest of this section for the sake of lucidity.

As it pertains to the competing definitions, I begin with Arash Abizadeh (2001) who points out that *ethnicity* is often used interchangeably with *race* as they are both usually defined in terms of "shared genealogy." Nonetheless, he says, *ethnicity* also includes shared behavioral, cultural, linguistic, or religious characteristics. Contrastingly, he adds, *race* denotes "some concentrations, as relative to frequency and distribution, of hereditary particles (genes) and physical characters, which appear, fluctuate, and often disappear in the course of time by reason of geography and/or cultural isolation" (Abizadeh, 2001, p. 23).

Next, according to Alfred Metraux (1950), in 1950, the United Nations Educational, Scientific, and Cultural Organization (UNESCO) report titled *The Race Question*, signed by some of the internationally well-respected scholars at the time, including Ashley Montague, Claude Levi-Straus, Gunnar Myrdal, Julian Huxley, and others, stated the following about the problem that arises when *ethnicity* and *race* are used interchangeably and a corrective:

> National, religious, geographic, linguistic and cultural groups do not necessarily coincide with racial groups; and the cultural traits of such groups have no demonstrated genetic connection with racial traits. Because serious errors of this kind are habitually committed when the term "race" is used in popular parlance, it would be better when speaking of human races to drop the term "race" altogether and speak of "ethnic groups." (Metraux, 1950, p. 142–143)

Also, we glean from Jeanne H. Ballantine, Keith A. Roberts and Kathleen Odell Korgen (2019) that *ethnicity* then hinges upon cultural features such as beliefs, customs, dress, foods, language, norms, values, a shared group identity or feeling, and sometimes loyalty to a homeland, monarch, or religious leader. Members are grouped together because they share a common cultural heritage that is often linked with a geographical or national identity. Ballantine, Roberts and Korgen further mention that some social scientists prefer the concept *ethnicity* over the concept *race* because the former comprises most minorities and eschews the problems with the latter.

In addition, one learns from the United States Census Bureau (2020) that collectives of related ethnic groups are typically referred to as "ethnic." The various Latin American ethnic groups plus a racial mix of the Spanish or Portuguese are typically referred to as, depending on the part of the United States they reside, either as "Hispanics" or "Latinos/Latinas." The many previously designated "Oriental" ethnic groups are referred to as Asian ethnic groups and similarly lumped together as "Asians." The concepts of "Black" and "African American," although different, are employed to describe the descendants whose ancestors, usually in predominant part, were indigenous to Africa. The term "White Americans" refers to peoples originally from Europe that now live in North America. "Middle Easterners" are people from the concocted Middle East: i.e., Southwest Asia and North America (U.S. Census Bureau, 2020).

An observer needs only visit Washington, DC's Adams Morgan, Chinatown and Georgetown neighborhoods to get a picture of *ethnicity* in the city. The person will see non-English street and store names, newspapers, ethnic restaurants, culture-specific houses of worship and clothing styles that reflect ethnic subcultures.

Furthermore, *ethnicity* has been denoted in terms of how internal conflicts in a country are precipitated by ethnic factors. Two major ethnic factors have been identified as triggers for the conflicts. The first one has to do with ethnic majorities exercising cultural discrimination against ethnic minorities. Cultural discrimination might include inequitable educational opportunities, legal and political constraints on the use of and teaching of minority languages, and constraints on religious freedom. In some cases, draconian measures to assimilate minority populations combined with programs to bring large numbers of other ethnic groups into minority areas constitute a form of cultural genocide (Brown, 1996).

The second major ethnic factor is apropos the utilization of histories and perceptions by a group of its own versus those of others. It is inevitable that many groups have legitimate grievances against others for crimes of one kind or another committed at some point in the distant or recent past. Some "ancient hatreds" have legitimate historical bases. Nonetheless, it is also true that groups tend to whitewash and glorify their own histories while demonizing either their neighbors or rivals and adversaries (Brown, 1996).

Indeed, these "ancient hatreds" can be quite troublesome if rival groups have mirror images of one another, which is often the case. For instance, when two groups in close proximity have reciprocally inflammatory views of each other, the slightest provocation on either side confirms deep held beliefs and provides the justification for retaliatory response. Under these circumstances, conflict is hard to avoid and even harder to limit, once started (Brown, 1996).

Concerning conceptualizing *ethnicity* as a social fact, the focus is on cases whereby ethnic groups cannot be distinguished from the bulk of the population by looking at their physical attributes. For instance, Irish, German, Polish and Russian Americans are often physically indistinguishable. Yet, members of these groups have been able to establish different subcultures based on their different ethnic backgrounds (Robertson, 1987).

Thus, from a sociological point of view, an *ethnic group* is a classification of people who, based on their shared cultural heritage, are regarded as socially distinct. In essence, unlike racial dissimilarities, ethnic distinctions are culturally learned and not genetically established. While this aspect appears obvious, we, nonetheless, see certain linguistic descriptors employed to characterize some groups as "intelligent" and industrious" and others as "lazy" and "warlike," as if the traits are "inborn." It is a verity, however, that no group possesses "inborn" cultural traits. Instead, a group acquires traits via socialization in its specific environment. For instance, while the Japanese in Japan and Japanese Americans share the same genetic heritage, they, nevertheless, display different cultural norms and values (Robertson, 1987).

Vis-à-vis the functionalist and the conflict perspectives on *ethnicity*, the two notions are used to conceptualize *ethnicity* as it relates to intergroup relations. Commencing with the functionalist perspective, first, the viewpoint attempts to explicate persistent social aspects in terms of their positive impacts on society as a whole. Functionalists postulate that social inequality can serve as a function of compensating scarce talents. It can therefore be expected that some ethnic inequalities are a common facet of societies; functionalists would then look for the manifestation of some social benefits. In practice, however, they would dismiss such reasoning and instead pay attention to the dysfunction, or negative impacts, which ethnic antagonisms have on society (Robertson, 1987).

Second, functionalist theorists proffer that a social attribute can be functional for one group but dysfunctional for other groups. Thus, in the long run, ethnic inequality will always tend to be dysfunctional, mainly because the practice denies society the opportunity to make full use of the talents of all of its members. Also, sooner or later, the situation is bound to provoke hostility and even violence. This was the case in the United States South when White Americans stoked ethnic antagonisms that led to the rebellions of enslaved Africans (Robertson, 1987).

Third, functionalist theorists suggest that a certain level of group consciousness and loyalty can be functional under particular circumstances. This is because most human groups tend to exhibit *ethnocentrism*—i.e., the proclivity to assess other cultures by the standards of one's own culture. Some barometer of ethnocentrism is almost unavoidable in any ethnic group. This is due to the fact that to most people, it is self-evident that their own attitudes, cultural practices, norms, religion and values are appropriate and right, whereas they may perceive those of other groups as bizarre, immoral, inappropriate, or peculiar. Within limits, ethnocentrism can be functional to ensure a group's survival, as the attendant attitudes can foster cohesion and solidarity among the group's members. The belief by a group of people that their collectivity and way of life are "best" will develop confidence and faith in their own cultural tradition, will discourage penetration by outsiders, and will unite them to pursue their common goals. The danger, however, is that under particular conditions, ethnocentric attitudes can precipitate the exploitation and oppression of other groups (Robertson, 1987).

Fourth, and finally, in general, the functionalist perspective on ethnic relations is not well-developed. This is because it can be employed to demonstrate why hostile relations may be dysfunctional but does not actually spell out why ethnic inequalities emerge in the first place (Robertson, 1987).

As for the conflict perspective, for starters, it is the notion that is used more frequently by sociologists to analyze ethnic inequality. According to proponents of this perspective, ethnic inequality has the same source as any other type of social stratification, since it emerges from competition among different groups for the same scarce resources: i.e., power, prestige, and wealth. The collectivity that emerges victorious becomes the dominant group and the losers become the minority groups (Robertson, 1987).

Next, for ethnic antagonisms and inequalities to emerge, three fundamental circumstances must exist. The first circumstance has to do with *identifiable groups*—i.e., two or more social groups must exist that can be recognized by their visible physical features or cultural practices. The second circumstance is *competition for resources*—i.e., rivalry exists among groups for scarce resources such as land, jobs, and power. And, the third circumstance is *unequal power*—i.e., one group makes good its claim over scarce resources at the expense of the other groups. This situation then leads to inequality becoming structured into a society (Robertson, 1987).

Also, based on the preceding circumstances, events unfold in quite a predictable manner. The more groups compete for scarce resources, the more negatively they will perceive one another. The dominant group develops a contemptuous perception about what it considers the inferiority of the minority groups and utilizes the belief to continue its domination. When the minority groups attempt to assert their interests, the dominant group sees it as a threat to its hegemony and further oppresses the minority groups (Robertson, 1987).

In addition, according to conflict theorists, disputes among ethnic groups are not actually about ethnic differences; instead, they are about the use of the differences to establish and preserve inequality in the competition for scarce resources. In essence, wherever different ethnic groups compete for the same resources, intergroup hostility will occur, especially if the groups remain unequal and one of them has the means to exploit or victimize the other groups (Robertson, 1987).

Finally, conflict theorists postulate that when subordinate ethnic groups gain greater equality with the dominant group, hostilities tend to subside. They also posit contrastingly that when minority groups remain relatively impoverished, antipathy will be greatest against them (Robertson, 1987).

AFRO-LATINO/A IDENTITY IN THE AMERICAS AND THE UNITED STATES

The concept of Afro-Latino America was introduced to the United States by political scientists Anani Dzidzienyo and Pierre-Michel Fontaine, both of whom conducted research in Brazil on Black social and political movements. In 1978, Dzidzienyo published his findings in his article, "Activity and Inactivity in the Politics of Afro-Latin America" (Andrews, 2018). In addition, he states that in 1980, Fontaine reported on "The Political Economy of Afro-Latin America" wherein he defined the term "Afro-Latino" to include "all regions of Latin America where significant groups of people of known African ancestry are found." According to Alford, in his article, "More Latinas Are Choosing to Identify as Afro-Latina" (2018), the terms "Afro-Latina" or "Afro-Latinx" are recent adaptions of the phrase Latino for anyone who chooses to remove gender binaries from his/her identity. Furthermore, it is used to describe descendants of Latin America with African roots simply as Black Latinos/as (Alford, 2018). In addition, The Afro-Latin@ Reader describes Afro-Latinos/as as "people of African descent in Mexico, Central and South America, and the Spanish-speaking Caribbean and by extension those of African descent in the United States whose origins are in Latin America and the Caribbean (Latorre, 2012, p. 5).

In Lao-Montes' article, "Afro-Latinidades and the Diasporic Imaginary" (2005), he explains that Latin America and the Caribbean are where people were first massively shipped from Africa South of the Saharan or Black Africa in the 16th Century. He states that these locations held the largest concentrations of people of African descent in the Americas. During Latin America's colonial period, about 15 times as many enslaved African were taken to Spanish and Portuguese colonies than to the United States. Today, about 130 million people of African descent live in Latin America, making up roughly a quarter of the total population of the region, according to estimates from the Project on Ethnicity and Race in Latin America (PERLA) (Telles, 2014). Furthermore, Afro-Latinos/as make up significant shares of the populations in some corners of Latin America. For instance, in Brazil, about half of the population is of African descent (Black or mixed-race Black). Also, in the Caribbean, Black Cubans make up about a third of that country's population. However, estimates of Afro-descent in the Dominican Republic range from about a quarter to nearly 90% of the population, depending on whether the estimates include those who identify as "Indio," a group that includes many non-Whites and mixed-race individuals with African ancestry (Gonzalez-Barrera, 2016).

As Alford (2018) states, there are millions of Afro-Latino/a people around the world, from Honduras to Puerto Rico to the Dominican Republic, who have hundreds of combinations of skin colors and hair textures. But for many of them, the unifying experience comes from their "visible Blackness." While some believe that identifying as Afro-Latino/a is a "personal choice," others argue that their identity has more to do with their physical traits such as skin color and hair texture.

The Pew Research Center is a nonpartisan think tank that conducts public opinion polling and demographic research as part of its social science research portfolio. In 2016, the Pew Research Center issued its first nationally representative survey and asked Latino/a-Americans if they identify as Afro-Latino/a. The survey found that one out of four Latinos/as in the United States identify as Afro-Latino/a (Pew Research Center, 2016). In addition, the Pew Research Center found that Latinos with roots in the Caribbean were most likely to identify as Afro-Latino/a. One-quarter of all United States Latino/a adults self-identify as Afro-Latino/a, Afro-Caribbean, or of African descent with roots in Latin America (Pew Research Center, 2016.)

Some observers have argued that culture is the main basis for self-identification as an Afro-Latino/a. In Valdez's article, "Political Participation Among Latinos in the United States: The Effect of Group Identity and Consciousness (2011)," the author refers to Afro-Latinos/as as people of Afro-Hispanic ancestry and that Afro-Hispanics are tied more to their culture of origin and express themselves through their language and culture. Duany argues in his article, "Reconstructing Racial Identity: Ethnicity, Color, and Class amongst Dominicans in the United States and Puerto Rico (1998)," that race and color have played a crucial role in the formation of the cultural identities of Caribbean immigrants in the United States. He states that Caribbean migrants, especially those coming from the Spanish-speaking countries of Cuba, Dominican Republic and Puerto Rico, tend to use three main racial categories Black, White, and mixed based primarily on skin-color and other physical characteristics such as facial features and hair texture. He adds that Dominican immigrants in the United States and Puerto Rico tend to be treated as "Blacks," although most of them do not define themselves as such (Duany, 1998).

Other observers have attempted to explain the racial designations for Afro-Latinos/as based on their skin color. According to Newby and Dowling in their article, "Black and Hispanic: The Racial Identification of Afro-Cuban Immigrants in the Southwest (2007)," Afro-origin immigrants from the Spanish-speaking Caribbean may find their adjustment to the United States racial classification system particularly challenging. Newby and Dowling also state that Afro-Cubans face a construction of blackness that differs from their country of origin. The United States historical reliance on a "one drop rule," which defines anyone with African ancestry as "Black," is not congruent with Caribbean racial designations that typically use an array of color and phenotypic descriptors based on both physical and social characteristics (Newby and Dowling, 2007). In addition, many factors such as skin color, hair textures, language, and social standing influence racial identification in the Caribbean, a process that varies considerably by country. In the Dominican Republic, for example, persons use the category "Black" to refer to Haitians. Dominicans tend to avoid the categorization "Black" (Negro) and instead use several skin color categories that are also dependent on an individual's social class. Thus, when Dominicans of African ancestry arrive in the United States, they often refuse the label "Black," as it does not fit with their understanding of blackness (Newby and Dowling, 2007).

Duany (1998) alludes to Omi and Winant (1994) who claim that perceived racial identity of individuals and groups does not necessarily coincide with their self-perception. Persons from Latin America are accustomed to phenotypes and social statuses rather than biological descent to define a person's racial identity, especially in the Spanish-speaking countries. For instance, on the Island of Hispaniola, the social construction of race and ethnicity is characterized by a strong reactive or oppositional identity compared to Haitians. Duany further notes that it is the sense of national pride and rejection of their own Negritude that many Dominican migrants bring with them. They must reevaluate their perspectives when they confront the United States model of racial stratification. Also, Duany states that Puerto Ricans use phenotype rather than hypodescent as the main criterion for racial identity.

In alignment with many Dominicans, Puerto Ricans tend to think of three main physical types as well-White, Black, and Mulatto-defined primarily by skin color, facial features, and hair texture. Whereas North Americans pay closer attention to national origin in defining a person's ethnic identity, Puerto Ricans give a higher priority to birthplace and cultural orientation. Also, Puerto Ricans do not consider racial identity as a question of biological descent but rather one of physical appearance. Therefore, a person of mixed racial background is not automatically assigned to the Black group in Puerto Rico. Rather, racial classifications depend largely on skin color and other visible characteristics such as the shape of the mouth, nose, and hair (Duany, 1998).

Rivera defers to Anani Dzidzienyo in her article, "From Trigueñita to Afro-Puerto Rican: Intersections of the Racialized, Gendered, and Sexualized Body in Puerto Rico and the U.S. Mainland, (2006)" when she asserts that the real problem for Afro-Latinos/as is successfully juggling the desire for common nationality with the struggle to attain legitimacy for their African identity. She states that unfortunately, blackness is represented in stereotypical roles, such as the servant, the drug dealer, the impoverished, the prostitute, raperos

(Rappers), reggae toneros, and Dominican immigrant. Also, blackness on the island is equated with slavery, inferiority, awkwardness, ignorance, uneducated, comical, hypersexuality, and of the underprivileged class. Furthermore, blackness is seldom acknowledged, praised, or used as a concept to empower people on the island of Puerto Rico. She believes that perhaps such a gradation of brownness from Brown to Black somehow legitimizes why so many visibly Black Puerto Ricans do not classify themselves as Black. Regardless of their ancestral makeup, whether they have strong African features or show evidence of more Spanish blood, many Black Puerto Ricans do not view themselves as strictly Black, but rather as a combination of races. Rivera further notes that many Afro-Latinos/as on the mainland deny their blackness and identify themselves as "Hispanic like their European Compatriots" (Cruz-Janzen, 2001, p. 172). Rivera (2006) contends that identity is not static; instead, it is a fluid process negotiated through cultural and social relations. In the United States, hybridity is negotiated across clear-cut binaries of race: Black/White; language: English/Spanish; and social relations: segregation/integration.

According to Higgins in "Afro-Latinos: An Annotated Guide for Collection Building (2007)," the term "Afro-Latino/a" is itself fraught with ambiguity. In Africana, the multi-volume encyclopedia edited by Anthony Appiah and Henry Louis Gates Jr., the term Afro-Latino/a refers to "the cultural experience of Spanish-speaking black people in what has become the territory of the United States" (Appiah & Gates, 2005). For Latin American and Latino/a studies scholars such as Anani Dzidzienyo and Suzanne Oboler, the term Afro-Latino/a includes those identified as or who self-identify as Black in Latin America and the Hispanophone Caribbean. A more popular United States understanding of the term describes the connection between Latino and African American communities in the United States, particularly in relation to Cuban Americans and Puerto Ricans on the East Coast, whose cross-cultural contacts and productions have been more widely disseminated.

According to Peter Wade (2005), in Afro-Latino affairs, darker shade Latinos/as can even become White "blanqueamiento" if they reach a certain social status. As noted by many scholars, Black identity is not absolute in matters of phenotypes or physical characteristics such as shade of skin color, facial features, and hair texture. Hence, being "Afro-Latino/a" is fluid and transcendent depending on the individual and/or his or her location.

In sum, whether in the United States, Spanish-speaking Caribbean, or in Latin America, various scholars have characterized the term "Afro-Latino/a" as Black people from Spanish-speaking countries. However, it is clear that the identity of being Afro-Latino/a changes depending on the socioeconomic standing of the individual's ability to negotiate his or her identity.

VIEWS OF ETHNICITY AND PIGMENTOCRACY IN THE LATINO COMMUNITY

Silvio Torres Saillant suggests the following: "Because of the overwhelming racial fusion of the Dominican population, one cannot speak of Blacks versus Whites or identify cases in which people align themselves politically along [the United States color lines]" (The Johns Hopkins University Press, 2000). Also, as the U.S. Office of Management and Budget (OMB), the department responsible for setting standards for federal data collection such as the U.S. Census stipulates that Latino/a or Hispanic is not a race but rather an aspect of ethnicity. According to this "official" classification system, Latinos/as may be of any race, meaning the ones the OMB enumerates in federal data: White, Black, Native American, Asian, or Native Hawaiian or Pacific Islander. In addition, there is a great deal of overlap between how color and race function in a cross-cultural comparison of the United States and the Hispanic Caribbean. Color is a racialized physical attribute that is often used in Latin America in ways similar to how North Americans use race to stratify and structure society and to value particular racialized bodies over others.

Clara E. Rodriguez affirms in her book, *Changing Race-Latinos, the Census, and the History of Ethnicity in the United States (2000)*, that scholars contend that in Latin America, "race" is more like a "social race" or an "ethnicity." She also states that race in Latin America has been quite different from the ancient view, in that it also implies a "pigmentocracy," a racist paradigm in which honor, status, and prestige are signaled by skin color and phenotype. Therefore, in Latin America, "race" is seen as a social construct and in the United States is seen it as a genealogical concept. Rodriquez points out that in the Spanish Caribbean and Latin America, ancestral "blood" is only one variable determining one's race. Moreover, race is not necessarily passed down from generation to generation, as is implicit in a system based on hypodescent or genetic inheritance. Furthermore, in Latin America, "race" is not always based on just color. Other physical and social characteristics such as facial features, hair textures, social class, dress, personality, education, linguistic identity, cultural modes of behavior, relation to the referent to the speaker and context are important for "racial classification" (Rodriguez & Cordero-Guzman, 1992; Sanjek, 1971). Consequently, a person who would be considered White in the Spanish Caribbean might be considered Black or non-White in the United States because of the color of his or her skin (Rodriguez, 2000).

In her work, *Race Migrations: Latinos and the Cultural Transformation (2012)*, Roth states that there are different ways of classifying race as different nations and cultures often have their own ways of dividing the world into racial categories and deciding how to assign people to each one. She contends that race is also an aspect of culture: "Just as different societies have different ways of understanding race and different ways of determining what races exist, concepts of race are one aspect of the cultural change that immigrants may experience in a new society" (Roth, 2012). For instance, in the Dominican Republic and other countries of the Hispanic Caribbean, many believe that the category "Black" is reserved for those whose ancestry is only African, with no racial mixture. In contrast, in the United States, there has been a long history of the "one-drop rule," a principle of hypodescent. This allows African ancestry to trump everything else and lead to a Black designation, regardless of how distant that ancestry.

Regarding socioeconomic status, Roth (2012) also states that social considerations influence racial classifications in the continuum model. In the Latino community, greater socioeconomic status, prestige, or social networks can lead to a "lighter classification," giving rise to the common expression that "money whitens." In addition, pigmentocracy is used to rank groups and individuals based on their skin color. Roth additionally notes that in both Puerto Rico and the Dominican Republic, it is common for a child to be nicknamed *la blanquita* or *el negrito*, not because she or he is objectively White or Black, but because she or he is the lightest or the darkest in the family, respectively. Roth further recognizes that "color has real consequences for social outcomes in the Caribbean just as it does in the United States" (Roth, 2012). Also, social status and color are closely related in both the Dominican Republic and Puerto Rico, leading some to describe those societies as pigmentocracies. The continuum model, whether viewed as race or color, in one of several cognitive structures leads Puerto Rico and Dominican societies to organize people into hierarchically ordered categories on the basis of socially designated physical or biological characteristics. Roth goes on to assert that in the binary United States scheme using the one-drop rule, "Black" became a broad, phenotypically diverse category, incorporating people of different skin tones, appearances, and fraction of Black ancestry. By contrast, "White" was associated with racial "purity," the narrow group of those deemed to be "untainted" by Black ancestry. Yet, for Puerto Rican and Dominican majorities, color or a continuum scheme is the more important form of social stratification (Roth, 2012).

In contrast, Stephen E. Cornell and Douglas Hartmann claim in their book, *Ethnicity and Race: Making Identities in a Changing World (2007)*, that race is not simply a label forced upon people. Rather, race is an identity that people accept, resist, choose, specify, invent, redefine, reject, actively defend, and so forth. The authors suggest that the identity involves an active "we" as well as a "they." "They" involve not only circumstances, but active responses to circumstances by individuals and groups, guided by their own preconceptions, dispositions, and agendas. In making these assertions, Cornell and Hartmann propose the following three basic factors in identity construction: (1) boundaries, (2) perceived position, and (3) meaning. Boundaries involve the construction and positioning of borders that separate groups from one another, including criteria used to determine inclusion or exclusion. A group's position is where group members are perceived to be relative to other groups in a stratified society. This position in the hierarchy is integrally related to the construction and maintenance of boundaries. Finally, group meaning includes an assignment (by others) or assertion (by the group) of what factors are associated with membership in a specific group. That is how group membership is interpreted by group members, as well as by others (e.g., "we are oppressed" or "they are a strong people").

In some circumstances, a group may have the power to define and assert its own identity, despite a differing identity assigned by outsiders. In other cases, structural or material circumstances may limit a group's freedom to define itself (Cornell & Hartmann, 2007). Cornell and Hartmann go on the state that across the United States, the labels Hispanic and Latino/a are used as physical descriptors to describe persons who are "Brown." However, as Rodriguez (2000) notes, the fact that Hispanic persons who appear phenotypically White are often referred to as "light-skinned" and not as White demonstrates the ways in which Latinos/Hispanics are continually racialized. Referring to the category "Latino/Hispanic" as an ethnic group may downplay the racial assumptions implicit in its daily use. However, in conceiving "Latino/Hispanic" as a "Brown race," the group has not only been racialized as non-White but also as non-Black. In this way, the fact that "Hispanic/Latino" has become linked to "brownness" leads to difficulties for Afro-Latinos/as who are Spanish speaking and phenotypically Black.

In the article, "Black Behind the Ears and Up Front Too? Dominicans in The Black Mosaic (2001)," Candelario declares that in the United States, racial identification has been categorized largely within a White/non-White dichotomy. Furthermore, historically, those of wholly European descent have been considered White, although not without a surprising degree of legal, political, and socioeconomic conflict. She contends that one ceases to be White when "one-drop-of-(African)-blood" is introduced into the family lineage: "Thus, to have African ancestry and to be black are synonymous" (Candelario, 2001). This systematization of what Marvin Harris calls "hypo-descent" has categorized Latin Americans and United States Latinos/as as "Not White." By definition, "Not White" has not necessarily meant "Black" where Latinos/as are concerned. Rather, it has meant some version of "Mestizo." Latinos/as who acknowledge or celebrate their African ancestry do not necessarily identify primarily as "Black" because to be Black is by definition to be "not Mestizo." The problem with a "Mestizo" based notion of Latino/a identity, then, is that it elides the fact of Black racial identity for many Latinos/as.

Candelario (2001) further notes that in Latin America, racial identification and racial identity are somewhat more fluid and operate on a continuum. For instance, in both the Dominican Republic and in the United States, the vast majority of Dominicans with some degree of visible African ancestry are categorized as "Indio" or "Indian" with qualifiers such as "oscuro" (dark) and "claro" (light). The last Dominican census that quantified racial identification was taken in 1960 and found that only ten percent of the nation's inhabitants were considered to be "Black." Recent work on Dominican responses to the United States Census has found that Dominicans in New York, the second largest Dominican city in the world, identify primarily as "other" in terms of race, with about 28 percent self-identifying as "Black." By contrast, nearly half of Washington, DC's 1,500 Dominican residents identified as Black in the 1990 Census. But even in the United States, identity amongst Afro-Latinos/as or Latinos/as of African descent can be complicated.

For instance, Dominicans in Washington, DC identify as Black nearly twice as often as Dominicans in New York City precisely because the Dominican community in DC is small, has origins in West Indian and United States origin African American communities in the Dominican Republic, took root in a segregated Southern city, and came of age during a large, economically and politically diverse African American community. As Hector Corporan puts it, they "didn't have a choice but to recognize their blackness" (Candelario, 2001). The lack of a large Dominican community "creates a discontinuity of all the racial classifications that we use in Santo Domingo, which has been transplanted in New York City, but here that disappears" (Candelario, 2001). That they continue to sustain an ethnic identity as Dominicans, or more generally, as Latinos/as despite lacking a broad community base, is sociologically noteworthy.

Candelario notes that in Washington, DC there was and continues to be an incentive for Black self-identification. In the District of Columbia, African Americans are a numerical majority, wield increasing political power, hold the vast majority of government posts and jobs, and occupy a diversity of socioeconomic statuses. For example, just outside DC, Maryland's Prince Georges County has the largest percentage of affluent Blacks in the country. The class stratification of the African American community in Washington, DC also serves as an incentive to assimilate into a Black racial identity (Candelario, 2001).

Indeed, a number of scholars have noted that ethnicity in the Latino community is very fluid and society does not grant darker complexion Afro-Latinos/as greater ability to advance socially and economically throughout the other Americas as well as in the United States. The factors that contribute to their self-identity, particularly "Black" identity, have varied widely in the existing perspectives. While existing views provide some examination of ethnicity and pigmentocracy for Afro-Latinos/as, they do not fully explain how ethnicity and skin-color (pigmentocracy) impact the political opportunities for dark-skinned self-identified Afro-Latinos/as.

DESCRIPTIVE REPRESENTATION AND ELECTABILITY OF DARK-SKIN SELF-IDENTIFIED AFRO-LATINOS/AS INTO POLITICAL OFFICE

It was John A. Garcia who suggested the following:

> Los latinos somos de muchas nacionalidades distintas. Pero, díme qué nombre prefiere y yo puedo calibrar nuestra afinidad como una familia más grande. Pues, quizas no pueda. El proceso de extenderse más allá de la familia, de patria, depende en las experiencias que compartimos y cómo nos entendemos y nuestras interacciones. Pero, primero, necesito definir a cual grupo pertenezco.

English Translation:

> Latinos are of many distinct nationalities. But tell me which name you prefer, and I can gauge our relationship in the larger family. Well, perhaps I cannot. The process of extending ones' identity beyond family and country depends on the experiences that we share, how we understand one another, and our interactions. But, first, I need to decide to which group I belong. (John A. Garcia, 2011, p. 45)

Identity politics has long played a significant role in the outcome of elections in the United States. For instance, during the Jim Crow era, many African Americans in the U.S. South saw electing Black candidates into political offices as a method to express national grievances and provide a platform to advance their social and economic agendas. Although the "one drop" rule was in effect, lighter-skin African Americans had a greater chance of being elected into political office at any level. For instance, out of the ten Black officials elected into the Senate, eight of them passed the "brown bag test" or were of mixed races such as Hiram Rhodes Revels whose mother was of Scottish descent, Blanche Bruce whose father was a White Virginia planter, former United States President Barack Obama whose mother was of English descent, and Kamala Harris whose mother is a Tamil Indian. However, the notion of identity and ethnicity or the "one drop rule" doesn't classify or categorize members of the Latino community as does the United States racial structure.

In his article, "Political Participation Among Latinos in the United States: The Effect of Group Identity and Consciousness (2011)," Valdez states that the United States ranks third behind Mexico and Colombia as the country with the largest Latin American-descent population. At 44.3 million, or 15 percent of the nation's total, Latinos/as represent the largest minority group in the United States (United States Census Bureau, 2006). This large and growing population is changing the United States demographic landscape. Stokes-Brown observes that identifying racially as Latinos/as significantly influences these individual voter decisions over those who identify as White or "some other race." Moreover, Latinos/as are more likely to cast a ballot in favor of a Latino/a over a non-Latino/a candidate. In contrast, Latinos/as who identify racially as White or "some other race" are less likely to do so. Stokes-Brown (2012) also finds that Latinos/as who express a panethnic group consciousness (that is, the perception that their fate is "linked" with that of other Latinos/as) are more likely to participate politically than Latinos/as who do not.

Valdez (2011) argues that those Latinos/as who identify as Latino/a do not always ascribe to a panethnic identity. For example, the 2007 Latino National Survey provides questions on Latinos/as racial identity (based on the United States Census) as well as on their "primary identity." Most respondents racially identify as White. When asked to identify their "primary identity," however, 44 percent of Latinos/as identify panethnically (e.g., Latino/Hispanic) while 47 percent identify themselves ethnically (e.g., Mexican).

Sanchez and Morin note in their article, "The Effect of Descriptive Representation on Latinos' Views of Government and of Themselves (2011)," that there has been a substantial increase in the number of Latino/a elected officials (LEOs) in the United States. Specifically, they note that between the 101st (1989–1990) and 110th Congresses (2007–2009), the total number of LEOs within the United States House of Representatives and Senate more than doubled, increasing from 11 to 27. Noting that the apparent growth in the number of LEOs is even more apparent at the state level between 1985 and 1995, the number of Latinos/as elected to state legislatures increased from 114 to 163. This trend steadily continued through 2003, when Latinos/as occupied 211 legislative seats (160 representatives, 51 senators), spanning across 80 percent of state legislatures throughout the nation.

Also, some observers point out that LEOs mobilize their electorate and enhance levels of Latino/a participation (e.g., Barreto, 2007; Barreto, Segura & Woods, 2004). Less understood, however, is whether the presence of Latino/a descriptive representatives can influence the political attitudes of Latino citizens toward government and perceptions of group identity (Panjtoja & Segura, 2003). These concepts are important for analysis, as feelings of inclusion and efficacy are necessary for improving levels of political involvement and establishing overall democratic legitimacy (Mansbridge,

1999), while dimensions of group identity serve as important resources that influence political behavior among racial and ethnic groups.

In studies of descriptive representation, some observers indicate that minority elected officials were more likely than their White counterparts to promote the policy interests of their respective groups at the national (Canon, 1999; Whitby, 2002; Kerr and Miller, 1997; Cameron, Epstein and O'Halloran, 1996; Tate, 2003; Welch and Hibbing, 1984; Bratton and Haynie, 1999; Swain, 1993; Hero and Tolbert, 1995 Preuhs, 2012) and local levels of government (Bratton, 2006; Eisinger, 1982; Stein, 1986; Mladenka, 1989; Kerr and Mladenka, 1994). Also, other observers show that descriptive representation leads to increased political activity among racial and ethnic minority communities (Gay, 2002; Banducci, Donovan and Karp, 2005; Barreto, Segura and Woods, 2004, and 2005; Bobo and Gilliam, 1990). For example, exploring mayoral races across several United States cities, Barreto (2007) finds that the mobilization of Latinos/as by co-ethnic candidates leads to higher rates of political participation.

In addition, some observers argue that descriptive representation leads to positive outcomes beyond substantive representation, including the representation of different points of view and interests in legislative bodies (e.g., Phillips, 1998; Mansbridge, 1999). These authors contend that historically disadvantaged groups benefit from seeing members of their communities in positions of power and that descriptive representation is needed to compensate for past and continued injustices toward marginalized groups (Phillips, 1998; Mansbridge, 1999). In addition, other authors say that co-ethnic representation influences the manner in which racial and ethnic groups view politics and government; however, there is reason to believe that the presence of a descriptive representative may also heighten a sense of group belonging and solidarity among racial and ethnic groups. One form of group identity that has been particularly useful in describing the persistent use of group-based cues by African Americans is linked fate.

Many observers point out that when minority candidates are on the ballot and campaigning for political office, race and ethnicity often become central to the coverage of the campaign (Gay, 2001). In some cases, the candidates themselves provide racial cues to prospective voters for perceived electoral benefits (JoneReeves, 1994; Ttaugott, Price & Czilli, 1993; Is, 1987; Jones & Clemons, 1993). The media may also highlight race in these elections, regardless of the cues provided by the candidates themselves. In either case, voters are provided with racial or ethnic cues that can impact election outcomes and promote a sense of political commonality or identity among minority voters.

Nonetheless, Latinos/as who identify as Black racially are less likely to perceive a sense of political commonality with other Latinos/as. The role of race for this segment of the Latino/a population may lead Afro-Latinos/as to perceive greater levels of commonality with African Americans than with other Latinos/as (Logan, 2003; Nicholson, Pantoja & Segura, 2005). This perception may also be partially due to Afro-Latinos/as being subjected to discrimination in Latin America and the United States by lighter-skinned Latinos/as (Wade, 1997; Andrews, 2004; Peña, Sidanius, and Sawyer, 2004; Logan, 2003; Nicholson, Pantoja and Segura, 2005), which can decrease perceptions of political commonality. Sanchez and Morin (2011) demonstrate in their work that panethnic-based representation leads to positive political outcomes as well, decreasing political alienation among Latinos/as. They reveal that descriptive representation has normative value beyond substantive representation for the Latino population. More specifically, their results suggest that the rise in descriptive representation has an influence on not only how Afro-Latinos/as view government and politics, but also how they feel about their relationship with other Latinos/as.

Hero (1992) offers a different perspective. He believes that Latinos/as may be a group in name (a nominal group) but not necessarily a politically identifiable group. He sees the lack of Latino/a political and related social-psychological identification within and between groups as a chief explanation for the lack of Latino/a political influence. In his book titled *Latinos and the US Political System: Two-Tiered Pluralism (1992)*, Hero states that individuals may perceive themselves to be members of a particular ethnic-racial group, but self-definitions emerge, at least primarily, or even solely, in response to social and political structures and policies. He also argues that the historical experiences of Latinos/as in the United States have diverged from those of most Anglo and other ethnic groups. The word "Anglo," as used in the Southwest, means Non-Hispanic White, including those Eastern and Southern Europeans who settled in the Northwest and Midwest in the late 19th and 20th Centuries. So, the identity of Latinos/as is "different" politically (Browning, Marshall & Tabb 1990; Meier & Stewart, 1991). In many ways, a theoretically intriguing aspect of understanding Latino politics may lie in its uniqueness or its "betweenness" relative to the dominant (Anglo or White) or other ethnic immigrant groups, on the one hand, and other minority groups, on the other. That uniqueness has made the study of Latino politics particularly difficult and elusive. Hero (1992) further argues that Latino politics lies between race and ethnicity, or race-ethnicity and class. Specifically, Hero reflects concerns for equality and community, the relation and tension between interests and values, and between symbols and substance.

Hero (1992) moreover contends that Latinos/as are in a disadvantaged position politically, socially, and economically in the United States. They fare considerably less well than non-Hispanic Whites and less well in some instances than African Americans on a variety of measures of political representation and socioeconomic status. Therefore, Latino politics is best understood through a perspective of a two-tiered pluralism. That is, because of historical, socioeconomic, and other factors, minority individuals and groups have largely been relegated to the lower social and political tier or arena. Despite the equal and political status of Latinos/as formally, distinct factors and processes have led to systematically lower political and social status.

Latinos/as are difficult to categorize in terms of self-identification. They seem to be more ideologically diffused than African Americans or non-Hispanic Whites; they lean toward liberal self-identification, although the tendency is not particularly strong. Over 85 percent of Latinos/as live in urban areas, a higher percentage compared to the United States population as a whole (Moore and Pachon 1985). Due to this urban concentration, the political significance of Latinos/as is likely to be strong in local government. In fact, more than 75 percent of the 4,004 Latino/as elected and appointed officials in the United States hold positions in various local governments such as municipalities, counties, special districts, and school districts (National Association of Latino Elected and Appointed Officials, 1990). Hero states that according to some scholars, ethnic groups voting is likely to be higher among members of the first generation, when a group is new to the city, and assimilation has not yet taken place. Also, ethnic voting is highest among members of the second and third generations because middle-class status, which takes several generations to develop, is a "virtual prerequisite for candidacy for major office; an ethnic group's development of sufficient political skill and influence to secure nomination also requires the development of a middle class" (Wolfinger, 1974, p. 49).

Garcia (1994) states that ethnicity and identity reflect self-choice in terms of how individuals place themselves within a group and ethnicity. Group identity and pan-ethnicity involve the social construction of identity which occurs within the respective groups and is influenced externally. Garcia further says that many scholars and popular literature have discussed race in terms of phenotypes, skin color, biological traits, ancestry and social structures, and that public polices like the "one drop rule" have reinforced the concept of race as most directly associated to skin color and some notion of racial categorization. On the other hand, ethnicity is commonly associated with ancestry or national origin.

Garcia (1994) also believes that the American understanding of race and ethnicity is strongly related to skin color and serves as an external influence on group identification. In Latino communities, the development of pan-ethnic grouping and identity becomes a means to expand the group, its scope, and national visibility. Thus, the outgrowth of "Hispanicity" or Latino-ness represents a strategic decision among activists to enlarge the community and, potentially, its political capital and resource base. According to Rodriquez (2000), Puerto Rico has a multiplicity of "racial categories" or distinctions: Black, Indigos, *triguenos, negroes, morenos*, and White or Spanish. Therefore, the United States scheme, which categorizes persons as White, Black, possibly White, not White, and not Black, leaves Puerto Ricans outside the racial order. Rodriquez asserts that race, ethnicity, and culture are interconnected in the Puerto Rican experience and inconsistent with the United States view of race and who fits into what category.

Like many Puerto Ricans, many other Latino subgroups are confronting issues of cultural and political identity and political orientation focused on the United States. Recent gains in electoral representation to city and state levels serve as indicators of political development in the Dominican community. Yet, there is support for a state of mind that remains engaged with one's own native country, while becoming acclimated to the norms and activities in United States society. Some researchers refer to this as "political duality." A person can harbor double loyalties and interests in both the home country and the "host" country. The various ethnic labels usually reflect class, national origin, nativity, racial identification, cultural traditions, and language use (Garcia et al., 1994; Patterson, 1975).

Popular notions of political involvement tend to describe Latinos/as as less active in the electoral arena than other groups in the United States. Lower voter registration and lower voter turnout rates characterize their less-than-active role. A major contributing factor to this historic pattern lies with the significant segment of the Latino/a population that is foreign-born and non-citizens. In addition, data indicate that Latinos/as participate less in campaigns and tend to donate less money to campaigns. Overall, the discussion of Latinos/as in the electoral arena has concentrated on their potential to play a significant role in electoral outcomes rather than determine who gets elected. While Barreto (2007) indicates that the mobilization of Latinos/as by co-ethnic candidates leads to higher rates of political participation in mayoral races, the percentages of Latinos who are both registered and voting remain much lower than those of other groups and significant gains do not seem visible. In fact, Latinos/as tend to be less politically interested and less aware of political events and information (Garcia, 1995). Correspondingly, with lower levels of political awareness and interest, there is lower electoral involvement. As Hochschild and Weaver put it, racial identity is simultaneously a sentiment, a worldview, a perspective and framework for political action. People with a strong racial identity are likely to look at the world through racial lens, to be acute aware of other people's race in social settings, to define their own interests in light of the situation of Blacks, and to invoke a racial connotation in interpreting complex situations and subtle interpersonal cues (Hochschild and Weaver, 2007).

Hochschild and Weaver (2007) also note the complicated relationship between skin-color and electability into political office. They reveal that African American elected officials were disproportionately light-skinned and that people with lighter skin were overrepresented among elected political elites. Their research is a survey of a nationally representative sample of Blacks that varied in terms of skin tone, platforms, and names of candidates in a hypothetical election for Senate to provide evidence for the impact of skin color on candidate favorability. The results show that the light-skin Black candidate prevailed over the darker opponent by 18 percentage points, a larger margin than any other treatment group received. The respondents also rated the light-skin Black candidate as being more intelligent, more experienced, and more trustworthy than the dark-skin opponent. Therefore, colorism (pigmentocracy) operates in the political realm in much the same way that it does in the socioeconomic realm. In addition, some political scientists have shown that individuals' social, economic and cultural characteristics link to their political views.

Several observers have pointed out that ethnicity and identity vary differently among Latinos/as in their community compared to the standard United States binary racial structure. The "one drop" rule does not identify or categorize any Afro-Latino/a of any phenotype; yet, according to some observers, panethnic and ethnic identity have helped to advance Latino/a electability into United States political office (DeSipio, 2006).

The notion of representation may be regarded as an effort by elected or other public officials to build more inclusive, deliberative and engaged relationships with the public (Orr & McAteer, 2004). Also, representation as a political principle is a relationship through which an individual or group stands for or acts on behalf of a larger group of people (Heywood, 2002). Nevertheless, there is extensive work that offers many different definitions of political representation and some authors agree that political representation consists of the articulation and presentation of political agendas of given groups by various actors in decision-making arenas and key social fora in democratic societies (Penock & Chapman, 1968). Cotta (2007) defines political representation as an institutionalized system of political responsibility realized through the free electoral designation of certain fundamental political organisms. Pitkins (1967) provides one of the most straightforward definition of political representation that to represent is simply to make present again. In this definitions, political representation is the activity of making citizens' voices, opinions and perspectives present in the public policy-making processes. Political representation occurs when political actors speak, advocate and act on behalf of others in the political arena. Pitkins (1967) maintains that in order to understand the concept of political representation, one must consider the different ways in which the term is used. She identifies at least four different dimensions of representation: (1) *formalistic*, (2) *symbolic*, (3) descriptive, and (4) *substantive representation*. Each concept provides a different approach of examining representation.

First, *formalistic representation* refers to the institutional arrangements that precede and initiate representation. Interest groups are of importance and advocate various versions of qualified deliberative democratic models (Young, 1999; Mansbridge, 1999, Squires, 2000). Second, symbolic representation refers to the extent that representatives "stand for" the represented with an emphasis on symbols or symbolization. Pitkins (1967) provides the example of a flag as a symbol representing a nation. Symbolic representation is concerned not with who the representatives are or what they do, but how they are perceived and evaluated by those they represent.

Symbolic representation has been shown to affect a number of important political attitudes and behaviors among minority populations. Feelings of political efficacy, interest in politics, confidence in government, and evaluations of government officials have all been shown to be higher under conditions of symbolic representation (Abramson, 1972). The conditions of symbolic representation have been shown to alleviate one of the most persistent gaps in politics: the 'Trust gap' has been shown to diminish significantly when minority groups are descriptively represented (Hero and Tolbert, 1995). Next, substantive representation is defined as "acting in the interests of the represented in a manner responsive to them" (Pitkin, 1967, p. 209). Although Eulau and Karps (1977) identify a variety of ways that representatives may act on behalf of the represented, the most common interpretation is that substantive representation refers to policy responsiveness or the extent to which representatives enact laws and implement policies that are responsive to the needs or demands of citizens.

While Pitkins (1967) considers *substantive representation* to be the most important dimension of representation and the heart of the representational relationship, others question its priority. For example, Wahlke (1971) observes that policy responsiveness receives too much emphasis given the evidence that citizens possess few coherent policy beliefs and that representatives are poorly informed about the policy preferences of citizens except in exceptional cases. Nevertheless, policy responsiveness continues to be considered the central aspect of representation by numerous writes. A variety of them have attempted to measure the impact of policy responsiveness both on overall public interests and on race and gender-based interests (Bullock, 1995; Reingold, 2000). Lastly, individual representatives "stand for" the represented by virtue of sharing similar characteristics with the represented such as race, sex, age, class, occupation, gender, ethnicity, or geographical area (Ahmed, 2017).

Typically, representation should mirror the composition of the represented in important respects. Women representing women can be seen as a form of direct participation in decision-making bodies. The question of Afro-Latino/as achieving individual representation therefore is simply about counting the number of them in political office and not examining what Afro-Latino/a representatives are saying.

Descriptive representation is a political continuum resource along which social cleavages are stratified. To reduce representational inequality, many governments, political leaders, social justice advocates, and researchers champion the concept of descriptive representation. Proponents of descriptive representation assert that those elected officials who share similar demographic and experiential characteristics of their constituencies have sufficient empathy to evaluate and construct representative policy (Young, 1990; Phillips, 1995; Mansbridge, 1999).

In this sense, political structures encourage representation by empathetic demographic insiders. In practice, descriptive representation attempts to improve inequitable social conditions by providing historically marginalized groups such as Afro-Latinos/as the opportunities to become political elites. In so doing, proponents assert that descriptive representation safeguards the interests of the disadvantaged. Addressing inequitable political representation, theoretical debates focus on the tenability and philosophy of descriptive representation as a governance solution, especially in light of the current state of disadvantaged group representation (Mansbridge, 1999). It therefore refers to both an ideal and a reality, with the ideal being the governance solution and the reality the degree to which legislative bodies represent the demographics and experiences of the citizenry.

Descriptive representation has been criticized on various grounds (Mansbridge, 1999). The most common criticism is that descriptive representation would not lead to substantive representation, since that demographic qualities bear little or no relationship to deliberative capabilities. Others argue that by over-emphasizing group differences through the claim of supra-representational abilities, descriptive representation erodes the bonds among legislators whose job is to produce policies for all rather than a demographic subset of their constituency (Phillips, 1995).

Other criticisms focus on the difficulties of implementing descriptive representation. Choosing which groups from a multiplicity of genders, races, ethnicities, religions, age groups, physical handicaps and social classes are worthy of descriptive representation could be so complex that random or arbitrary assignment to legislative bodies is the only thing representing as an 'act for' and 'in the interest of' (Pitkins, 1967). By substantive representation, it is understood that "the representative, independent of physical or other characteristics, serves the interests of the community that he or she represents" (Diaz, 2005, p. 14).

As the Black Latino/a population in the United States, and particularly Washington, DC grows, greater attention is required as it relates to political representation in a climax where gentrification is taking place. The increasing number of Afro-Latinos/as raises questions about how members of this group understand their political positions. Descriptive representation, as used in this work, helps to explain the benefits of having elected officials who share similar demographic and characteristics with their constituencies.

IDENTIFYING THE LIMITATIONS IN THE COMPETING PERSPECTIVES

The competing perspectives on the topic regarding Afro-Latino/a identity in the Americas and the United States highlights the arguments made by scholars to identify the characteristics of being Afro-Latino/a on the basis of phenotypes, ie., skin color, hair texture and facial features which can be seen as being inclusive of an Afro-Latino/a identity. For instance, as Alford (2018) states, there are millions of Afro-Latino/a people around the world, from Honduras to Puerto Rico to the Dominican Republic, who have hundreds of combinations of skin colors and hair textures. But as he highlights, for many of them, the unifying experience comes from their "visible Blackness." However, the "visible Blackness" in physical appearance or as authors Newby and Dowling (2007) state historical reliance on a "one drop rule," which defines anyone with African ancestry as "Black," in the United States is not congruent with Caribbean racial designations that typically use an array of color and phenotypic descriptors based on physical characteristics. However, these viewpoints failed to capture that many self-identified Afro-Latinos/as do not possess the stereotypical black features and physical characteristics. Throughout the Americas and United States and particularly in Washington, DC, many self-identified Afro-Latinos/as possess some or European features as well which this work attempts to capture. This gap leaves open the viewpoints that only self-identified physically black Latinos/as have better insight to determine what social/racial factors influence the electability of light-skin and dark-skin self-identified Afro-Latinos/as running for political office in Washington, DC while less physically black Latinos/as are excluded. In addition, for example Dominicans tend to avoid the categorization "Black" (Negro) and instead use several skin color categories that are also dependent on an individual's social class. Thus, when Dominicans of African ancestry arrive in the United States, they often refuse the label "Black," as it does not fit with their understanding of blackness (Newby and Dowling, 2007).

As the competing perspectives highlight, some observers have argued that culture is the main basis for self-identification as an Afro-Latino/a. In Valdez's article, "Political Participation Among Latinos in the United States: The Effect of Group Identity and Consciousness (2011)," the author refers to Afro-Latinos/as as people of Afro-Hispanic ancestry and that Afro-Hispanics are tied more to their culture of origin and express themselves through their language and culture. She believes that perhaps such a gradation of brownness from Brown to Black somehow legitimizes why so many visibly Black Puerto Ricans do not classify themselves as Black. Regardless of their ancestral makeup, whether they have strong African features or show evidence of more Spanish blood, many Black Puerto Ricans do not view themselves as strictly Black, but rather as a combination of races. Rivera further notes that many Afro-Latinos/as on the mainland deny their blackness and identify themselves as "Hispanic like their European Compatriots" (Cruz-Janzen, 2001, p. 172). Rivera (2006) contends that identity is not static; instead, it is a fluid process negotiated through cultural and social relations. In Africana, the multi-volume encyclopedia edited by Anthony Appiah and Henry Louis Gates Jr., the term Afro-Latino/a refers to "the cultural experience of Spanish-speaking black people in what has become the territory of the United States" (Appiah & Gates, 2005). However, Roth (2012) also states that social considerations influence racial classifications in the continuum model. In the Latino community, greater socioeconomic status, prestige, or social networks can lead to a "lighter classification," giving rise to the common expression that "money whitens." The scholars in this book made compelling arguments to capture Afro-Latino/a identity based on physical appearance and cultural experiences, however a lot of research was composed to capture the Afro-Latino/a identity regarding a socioeconomical status where in many Latin American countries and in the United States "money whitens."

The scholars in this book make significant contributions to the viewpoints regarding ethnicity and pigmentocracy in the Latino community as they highlight factors such as racial fusion and economic status that contribute to one's identity in the Latino community. However, the arguments are discussed mostly regarding individuals or people in the Spanish speaking Caribbean, ie., Puerto Rico and Dominican Republic. Other observers have attempted to explain the racial designations for Afro-Latinos/as based on their skin color. According to Newby and Dowling in their article, "Black and Hispanic: The Racial Identification of Afro-Cuban Immigrants in the Southwest (2007)," Afro-origin immigrants from the Spanish-speaking Caribbean may find their adjustment to the United States racial classification system particularly challenging. Newby and Dowling also state that Afro-Cubans face a construction of blackness that differs from their country of origin. The United States historical reliance on a "one drop rule," which defines anyone with African ancestry as "Black," is not congruent with Caribbean racial designations that typically use an array of color and phenotypic descriptors based on both physical and social characteristics (Newby and Dowling, 2007). This gap fails to capture the essence of the hypothetic question which I will restate: What social/racial factors influence the electability of light-skin and dark-skin self-identified Afro-Latinos/as running for political office in Washington, DC? This book attempts to close the gap and answer the question.

Also, other observers show that descriptive representation leads to increased political activity among racial and ethnic minority communities (Gay, 2002; Banducci, Donovan and Karp, 2005; Barreto, Segura and Woods, 2004, and 2005; Bobo and Gilliam, 1990). For example, exploring mayoral races across several United States cities, Barreto (2007) finds that the mobilization of Latinos/as by co-ethnic candidates leads to higher rates of political participation.

Sanchez and Morin note in their article, "The Effect of Descriptive Representation on Latinos' Views of Government and of Themselves (2011)," that there has been a substantial increase in the number of Latino/a elected officials (LEOs) in the United States. Specifically, they note that between the 101st (1989–1990) and 110th Congresses (2007–2009), the total number of LEOs within the United States House of Representatives and Senate more than doubled, increasing from 11 to 27. Noting that the apparent growth in the number of LEOs is even more apparent at the state level between 1985 and 1995, the number of Latinos/as elected to state legislatures increased from 114 to 163. This trend steadily continued through 2003, when Latinos/as occupied 211 legislative seats (160 representatives, 51 senators), spanning across 80 percent of state legislatures throughout the nation.

In addition, other authors say that co-ethnic representation influences the manner in which racial and ethnic groups view politics and government; however, there is reason to believe that the presence of a descriptive representative may also heighten a sense of group belonging and solidarity among racial and ethnic groups.

Descriptive representation focuses more on women rather than ethnic groups. And when a work discusses ethnic groups, it focuses on United States Black women instead of Black Latinos/as. Therefore, there is not a lot of work regarding descriptive representation in relations to the Afro-Latino/a community. Unfortunately, this gap in the existing works communicates the problematic message that (a) race and ethnicity are mutually exclusive, and (b) that the experience of Afro-Latinos/as in Washington, DC is representative of Afro-Latinos/as across the United States. The gap leaves open the room to challenge a one-sided analysis of how and why Afro-Latinos/as come to view the electability of light-skin and dark-skin self-identified Afro-Latino/a into political office.

Chapter 3

Afro-Latino/a Identity and Electability

The results dealing with the first major research question of the study is analyzed in this chapter. To restate the question, what social/racial factors influence the electability of light-skin and dark-skin self-identified Afro-Latinos/as running for political office in Washington, DC? Due to the fact that this study is qualitative, the rest of the chapter is divided into three sections. The first section provides a conceptual discussion on ethnicity; the second section discusses the qualitative results and the third section provides an analysis of the findings and determines the validity of the hypothesis of the major research question stated above. In addition, the names of the interviewees were modified to conceal their identity for this study. Before doing all this, however, some background information on the topic broached in this chapter is provided.

During the historic presidential primary of 2008, Barack Obama, a bi-racial man, ran against Hillary Clinton, a White woman; after contentious debates, Obama became the United States' Democratic Party candidate. He later became the President after successfully defeating the White Republican candidate, Senator John McCain, for the 45th presidency. For the first time in history, the American citizens elected someone other than a White male to the U.S. presidential office. This monumental event, along with the demographic shifts changing the face of the United States from a mostly White to increasing non-White nation, gives concrete hope that racial attitudes are changing and will move toward a more inclusive politics. But, as Nicholas De Genova (2005) has argued, nativist and racist attitudes persist and are ingrained in society, despite the tremendous growth of immigrant populations from Asia and Latin America that have contributed to the current multicultural image of the United States. The popularity of, for example, Latin music and food is often called on as evidence of the United States' greater acceptance of difference. However, as cultural studies scholar Lisa Lowe explains, ethnic differences are aestheticized by the nation through a celebration of "multiculturalism" to absolve the United States from thoroughly addressing the problem of race (Lowe, 1996).

One of the problems is the persistence of the conception of "race" as fixed or essential, and the rigidity of the Black/White binary evident in the categorization of Obama, the son of a White American woman and a Black African man, as "Black" in the media. Similarly, it is strongly illustrated in the current experiences of Black Latinos/as in the United States, where blackness is the most prominent characteristic used to "other" them. Moreover, the combination of African features with a Spanish accent makes Afro-Latinos/as exotic, not only for many Whites, but for many African Americans and other United States Latinos too. Most notably, Afro-Latinos/as' experiences differ from those of other people of African descent, i.e., Afro-Caribbeans and Afro-Europeans because of the ways in which many non-Black people in the Latino communities isolate and associate them with other Black Americans instead of persons of their own community. As this chapter makes clear, Afro-Latinos/as' responses to attempts to classify and contain themselves show how their multiple identities (Black, Afro-Latino/a, and Latino), as well as their negotiations of United States racial structures, challenge predominant racial paradigms.

The fact that many Afro-Latinos/as are often confronted with questions about their identities forces many of them to think about race and its complexity in ways that differ from people whose identities do not frequently come into question. So, how do these complexities play out in the political arena? Do certain ideologies impact the way Afro-Latinos/as view themselves as well as Afro-Latino/a political candidates? This chapter seeks to address the aforementioned questions in addition to the major research question stated earlier. Also, in order to provide a theoretical backdrop for the findings in the section entailing the qualitative results on the preceding questions, I will first discuss the notion of *identity* on which the findings are pegged.

IDENTITY: A BRIEF THEORETICAL DISCUSSION

For starters, *identity* generally means the fact of being who or what a person or thing is. It also denotes a close similarity or affinity. In discussing the theoretical underpinnings of *identity*, political scientists (examples: Huddy, 2001; Smith, 2004), like other social scientists, draw from the field of Psychology. I do the same here. But before delving into the theoretical postulates of *identity*, I will first discuss how it is shaped during the early stages of life and in moral development, which are among the major attributes that underlie how a political candidate identifies himself/herself in order to gain electability.

Beginning with how *identity* is shaped during the early stages of life, we learn from Jonathan L. Freedman (1982) that a phenomenon that has a very powerful effect on children's development and intensifies their early relationships is a strong tendency for them to emulate the behavior, beliefs and mannerisms of an adult and to consent to whatever the adult says. This combination of affection, close copying, love and respect shapes a child's *identity*. Children shape themselves after a figure in their environment. In the early stages of the life a child, the adult is frequently the mother; nonetheless, the person can also be another mothering adult or the father if he plays a more discernible role. Whoever the adult person may be, his/her (or a small number of adults) continuing presence in the child's life appears to be very significant in the child's normal development. This model is utilized by children so that they can shape their own behavior and personality and to also do what is expected of them in the world. Accordingly, the absence of an adult appears to leave children confused, low in self-awareness and self-esteem, and lacking a clear sense of morals and values (Freedman, 1982).

Also, evidence is shown to exist which indicates that when children are deprived of a consistent adult early in their lives, they suffer tremendously. Children who are separated from their parents and placed in hospitals or nurseries for long periods of time become agitated and depressed. This was the case during World War II of those English children who were moved out of London to protect them from bombing and placed in centers that lacked one permanent adult. While children can adapt reasonably well to brief separations, they suffer seriously when they are separated from their mothers or some permanent substitutes for extended periods (Freedman, 1982).

In addition, the preceding observation is not to assert that the traditional family arrangement is the only manner that an allowable adult model can be established. For example, on the *khibutz* ("collective farm") in Israel, children are raised collectively. After birth, infants on the *khibutz* are placed in a nursery instead of with their parents. The mothers have the responsibility to care for and feed their children during the first year; after that, the responsibility shifts to specially-trained people at the community nursery. The mothers do visit their children during the evenings and weekends. The substitute mothers spend a great amount of time with the children and it is their sole responsibility on the farm. The obvious advantages of this arrangement include guarantee expert care and efficiency, and relief for the mothers of child rearing responsibilities which allows them to actively participate in farming activities. Nonetheless, this arrangement raises the issue about whether the "collective motherhood" of this nature will produce healthy children. This is because no matter how well trained and dedicated a substitute mother is, sharing her time with a large number of children will not allow any one child to get the amount of love she/he would ordinarily receive from his/her mother. Nevertheless, as stated earlier, mothers on the *khibutz* do spend time with their children in the evenings and weekends, which is comparable or more than the amount of time working mothers spend with their children in the United States (Freedman, 1982) and many other developed countries.

Nonetheless, studies that have been done on children on the *khibutz* have yielded mixed results. While some researchers found that children on the *khibutz* were slightly behind in terms of mental development compared to children raised in non-collective environments, other researchers discovered that there were no differences between them. Such comparisons, however, are quite problematic as life on the *khibutz* is different in many ways compared to that in non-collective communities. A study attempted to show the differences between the two types of communities by comparing the children on the *khibutz* and those on the *mosharim* (more correctly singular *moshav* and plural *moshvim*—i.e., "cooperative agricultural settlement" and "settlements" governed by an elected council), which does not raise children in a communal manner. The findings were that the children on the former community had higher *identity* with their parents, higher self-esteem, and more social interests compared to the children in the latter community (Freedman, 1982).

Furthermore, while the research findings are inconclusive, they do, however, suggest that raising children collectively with a trained, affectionate and dedicated substitute mother has some advantages and does not necessarily yield manifest inadequacies. In sum, the findings demonstrate that claims of community child care centers having harmful effects on children should not be accepted willy-nilly (Freedman, 1982).

Finally, it is worth mentioning that one outcome of *identity* children develop based on an adult is the emergence of their *sexual identity*. Freedman explains this phenomenon as follows: "Young children learn to behave 'appropriately' for their sex through a process of reinforcement and identification with the same-sex parent. This sexual identification has an enormous effect on most children, which endures throughout their lives. The process by which it occurs is . . . that children adopt the behavior and values of the parent, but identification is concentrated on the parent of the same sex" (1982, p. 372).

Next, in terms of moral development, Freedman apprises us that *identity* has a significant effect on the process, as it propels children to accept the morality of an adult. In addition to learning what that morality is, children are also exposed to many various notions of morality. But once children have taken up an *identity*, they tend to pattern themselves after the adult from whom the identity is derived. In fact, some observers have pointed out that children who do not receive consistent adult connection, or who are so terribly treated that they do not develop an *identity*, tend to develop a fragile or warped sense of morality. People with a morality are usually referred to as "psychopaths." They feel no guilt for their negative actions, and they have a high propensity to violate established rules. While other factors do contribute to shaping the psychopathic behavior of an individual, one of the most significant contributing factors to the behavior is the absence of *identity* caused by the absence of a sense of morality (Freedman, 1982).

With this backdrop, I can now examine and provide a good understanding of the theoretical postulates that have been tendered to explicate *identity*. From the theoretical investigations of the concept, at least the following five seven postulates can be discerned: (1) career decision identity, (2) group identity, (3) identity foreclosure, (4) identity status, (5) individual versus role diffusion identity, and (6) sex differences formation identity. They are discussed in the ensuing paragraphs in the sequential order they are stated here for perspicuity.

First, the proposition put forward by proponents of *career decision identity* is that it is the fundamental means via which identity is expressed in society as a commitment to an occupation. This is increasingly becoming the norm for both males and females. Occupational choice is increasingly being aligned with sex-role identity, as well as education and aspirations, abilities and educational background, and situational circumstances that affect the job market at the time a person seeks employment (Newman and Newman, 2017).

Also, a model of career decision making has been proposed to explain *career decision identity*. The goal is said to hinge upon a number of distinct quests during adolescence and early childhood. Armed with effective problem solving skills, a person gains increased control over life events and is better situated to tackle the problems of the subsequent stage of decision making. Theorists propounding *career decision identity* suggest the following seven stages in the process, with the first four stages emphasizing planning and clarification, and the last three stages emphasizing implementation (Newman and Newman, 2017; Miller and Tiedeman, 1972; Tiedeman and O'Hara, 1963):

1. *Exploration stage* involves a person becoming aware of the fact that a decision must be made. This reality forces the person to learn more about his/her own self and the world of work. With a feeling of anxiety and uncertainty about the future, the person begins to engender alternatives for action (Newman and Newman, 2017; Miller and Tiedeman, 1972; Tiedeman and O'Hara, 1963).
2. *Crystallization stage* is when the person becomes more knowledgeable about the alternatives for action and their attendant effects. This leads to the recognition of the conflicts among alternatives, in turn leading to some of them being rejected. A cost-benefit evaluation is done among the remaining alternatives, and the person develops the criteria for

selecting the best alternative (Newman and Newman, 2017; Miller and Tiedeman, 1972; Tiedeman and O'Hara, 1963).

3. *Choice stage* is the phase during which the person makes a decision about which alternative for action will be selected. As the selected alternative is solidified in the person's mind, she/he develops detailed rationalities for why the alternative is worthwhile. The person then commits himself/herself to bringing the alternative to fruition (Newman and Newman, 2017; Miller and Tiedeman, 1972; Tiedeman and O'Hara, 1963).

4. *Clarification stage* involves the person developing a fuller comprehension of the effects of the commitment to the alternative selected. The person then plans the steps to be taken for the action to be implemented. At this stage, the action may be implemented or postponed to a later stage. It is also at this stage that the person prepares his/her self-image for modification based on the decision (Newman and Newman, 2017; Miller and Tiedeman, 1972; Tiedeman and O'Hara, 1963).

5. *Induction stage* is the phase during which the person comes up against the new environment for the first time, as she/he desires to be accepted and looks to others for signals on how to behave in that milieu. While identifying with the new group, the person also seeks acknowledgement for his/her distinctive attributes. As times goes on, the person modifies his/her self-image in line with the new environment. The person also learns to believe in the goals and values of the new group (Newman and Newman, 2017; Miller and Tiedeman, 1972; Tiedeman and O'Hara, 1963).

6. *Reformation stage* is the juncture where the person strongly embraces the new group. The person becomes more self-assured and asks that the group does its tasks better. She/he also seeks to convince group members to acclimatize some of his/her own values. As the person is perceived by group members as being strongly committed to the group's goals and values, these aspects may be modified to include his/her own (Newman and Newman, 2017; Miller and Tiedeman, 1972; Tiedeman and O'Hara, 1963).

7. *Integration stage* is when members oppose the new person's efforts to sway the group. The new member would then seek a compromise, which would lead him/her to get a more objective comprehension of self and group. This would also make it possible for the new member and the group to manifest true collaboration. It would further make the new member satisfied and evaluates himself/herself as successful and by group members as well (Newman and Newman, 2017; Miller and Tiedeman, 1972; Tiedeman and O'Hara, 1963).

Clearly evident in the *career decision identity* model is the prominence assigned to the continued interaction between the individual and the work setting. For starters, interaction is imperative for clarifying a person's talents and career choice. Thereafter, interaction is mandatory for achieving a satisfactory level of adaptation to the work setting. Thus, all of the preceding seven stages of *career decision identity* are pivotal for making an effective career-related decision, which includes choices involving a college major, occupation, job change, and career redirection (Newman and Newman, 2017).

Indeed, anyone engaged in the process of choosing a career is most likely to deal with the aforementioned seven stages of decision making. Nonetheless, people employ different styles of decision making that dictate how they utilize the information they receive and how much responsibility they take for reaching their decisions (Newman and Newman, 2017). Barbara M. Newman and Philip R. Newman (2017) mention Harren (1976) as having described the following three categories of styles for making such decisions: (1) "planning," (2) "intuitive," and (3) "dependent." Newman and Newman then go on to explicate these styles as follows:

> The planning style is the most rational. Planners assume personal responsibility for a decision. They seek out information to assess both personal competencies and the qualities of the situation. The intuitive style makes primary use of fantasy and emotion. A decision is reached without much information seeking. It is based on what feels right or best at the time. The dependent style is influenced by the expectations and evaluations of others. Dependent decision makers take little responsibility for their decisions. They see circumstances as forcing their decisions or limiting their options. (Newman and Newman, 2017, p. 354)

Second, *group identity* theorists focus on two aspects: (1) the conflict that emerges from sources of the pressure to join groups and (2) the resolution of the conflict. Starting with the first aspect, it is proffered that a psychosocial conflict with which we must confront as we transition from childhood to adolescence is *group identity versus alienation*. At this stage, we experience a significant amount of pressure to affiliate with a group of peers. The three sources from where the pressure emerges are (1) family, (2) age-mates, and (3) school (Newman and Newman, 2017).

In the case of the family, between the ages of 13 and 14, adolescents begin to spend long periods of time away from home. When they become high school students, they may spend more time in school activities, with schoolmates after classes, or on a job. During the evenings and the weekends, the children may attend school functions, go out on dates, or spend time with friends. Those children who can afford to own a car or have access to one may be away from home even more and at faraway places. When their children become adolescents, parents find it very difficult to plan meals and other events for the entire family. The children's increased mobility and involvement in activities away from home also mean fewer opportunities for parents to directly guide their children than they did previously (Newman and Newman, 2017).

As it pertains to age-mates, parents become quite worried about the other adolescents with whom their children spend time and the types of activities in which they engage. The worries make parents to ask their children about their friends, and some of the questions may seem condemning and intrusive to some children. Some parents may discourage or forbid their children from making friendships with other children or participating in activities they perceive to be harmful to or inappropriate for their children. Also, some parents may do the complete opposite and encourage their children to make friendships and participate in activities with other children that they perceive to be good. In essence, there will be minimal conflict about friendships when an adolescent's peer associations mirror the parents' goals and values (Newman and Newman, 2017; Petroni, 1871).

Apropos school, adults both passively accept and actively encourage the organization of peer groupings for and by students. In a passive framework, adults accept the friendship groups as they exist in the school and do very little to bring members of different peer groups to work with those in a particular group. They permit students to establish areas of cooperation among themselves, but also boundaries and rivalries in their relationships. In an active framework, adults strengthen some attributes of the peer groups by choosing certain students for particular roles. In fact, school adults accept the peer group structure and make almost no attempt to change it, which they recall from their own school days (Newman and Newman, 2017).

Next, vis-à-vis the resolution of the conflict, children during their early adolescence look for membership, which involves an internal probing about the group to which they are most interested to be a part. While membership in a peer group may be the more pressing issue to adolescents, other issues about group identification also exist. Adolescents may seek a commitment to a particular organization, they may assess the nature of their relationships with immediate or extended family members, and they may begin to comprehend the unique features of their neighborhoods or community. Also, while they are seeking group affiliation, adolescents must deal with the fit or lack of fit between their personal necessities and the values held by relevant social groups in their surroundings. Within the context of the substantive groups that exist for identification, individual needs for social approval or affiliation also occur. During early adolescence, individual necessities for social approval or affiliation, for status or reputation, and for power and leadership are either accepted or rejected (Newman and Newman, 2017). Resolution of this conflict can be either positive or negative.

Resolving the conflict between *group identity* and alienation involves adolescents believing that an existing group provides them with a sense of belonging and meets their social needs. The sense of belonging and needs fulfillment provide psychological growth for adolescents and also help them to integrate the necessary developmental tasks during the early stage of their adolescence (Newman and Newman, 2017).

In terms of the occurrence of a negative resolution to the conflict, adolescents are left with a sense of alienation. They experience no sense of belonging to a group and become quite uneasy in the presence of their peers. A precipitator of this outcome is when parents pressure their children to restrict their association to a particular peer group, but the group rejects their request for membership. Another causal factor is when adolescents look for membership in a group that meets their needs, but none exists. Consequently, these adolescents will not be members of any group. One more causal factor is that no peer group offers membership to certain adolescence, leading them to be shut out of all the social groups in their surroundings (Newman and Newman, 2017).

Third, *identity foreclosure* is the postulation that a person resolves an identity crisis by making a series of premature decisions about his/her identity often in response to the demands made by other people. For instance, early in their adolescence stage, young people may decide to become what their parents or grandparents wish them to become. These adolescents never question this decision apropos their developing personality. They could also become so unyielding in their commitment to such decisions that they do not identify the specific ways in which the decisions buttress their own egos (Newman and Newsman, 2017; Marcia, 1980).

Fourth, *identity status* theorists put forward the proposition that the phenomenon underlies the essence and, thus, the analysis of career decision making. Their thesis is that some degree of experimentation is needed so that an identity achievement is attained in an environment. Accordingly, they say that a period of questioning and indecisiveness is characterized as a temporal trait of a positive developmental process. For example, a college setting is a place where occupational identity can be built up quite slowly, even though indecisiveness is uncomfortable and pressure exist to reach closure quickly (Newman and Newman, 2017).

Also, *identity status* theorists suggest two different levels of the phenomenon that can lead to the expression of indecision. One of these levels is *moratorium*—i.e., a temporary prohibition of an activity. At this level, individuals have low career saliency and could benefit by continued exposure to alternative choices and by opportunities to experiment with different occupational roles. The other level is *diffusion*—i.e., the spreading of something more widely. Here, the reason for *diffusion* is said to be self-uncertainty. Individuals who fall into this category tend to need more information, have trouble defining themselves, and find it difficult to make choices or recognize their abilities (Newman and Newman, 2017; Jones and Chenery, 1980).

Fifth, the theory of *individual versus role diffusion identity* is derived from the work of Erik Erikson (1950, 1959a, 1959b, 1968 & 1974). A full discussion of his perspectives is beyond the scope of this section and not necessary. What I restate here very briefly are the two cardinal points in his work.

One cardinal point in Erikson's work is that identity is shaped by the amalgamation of past identifications, present-day cultural realities, and future aspirations. Another cardinal point is that as adolescents develop, they become preoccupied with matters pertaining to their essential character in the same manner they were preoccupied with matters of their origin during their early school days. Thus, as they seek to define themselves, later adolescents take into consideration the bonds that had been built with others in the past, in addition to the direction they wish to take in the future (Erikson, 1950, 1959a, 1959b, 1968 & 1974; see also Newman and Newman, 2017).

Sixth, and finally, *sex differences formation identity*, which concerns issues that have been raised about the process of identity formation and its end result for young men and women, has led to the development of three competing schools of thought. One school contends that the manner in which the concept of *identity* has been formulated is a reflection of a male-oriented culture that pays greater attention to ideology and occupation instead of interpersonal commitments. Another school proffers that the process of identity formation is different for young women because they must reconcile issues dealing with intimacy and interpersonal commitments before they can achieve closure to the world of work. The other school posits that rather than assume a proactive stance on identity formation, women are socialized to look to others in order to define their identity (Newman and Newman, 2017; Ginsberg and Orlofsky, 1981).

In sum, the perspectives of the three schools mirror the impact of the traditional differences in the male and female sex roles. Nonetheless, it has also been observed that for the adaptive functioning of men and women, the kinds of ego strengths connected with identity formation are just as imperative. Consequently, we can expect to find dissimilarities between males and females in the content of identity-related commitments, albeit not in the process of crisis and commitment (Newman and Newman, 2017; Ginsberg and Orlofsky, 1981).

QUALITATIVE RESULTS

One of the first people interviewed for this project was Ed, a 50-year-old man living in Washington, DC who came to the District of Columbia from Central America in the early 2000s. When asked about how he would describe himself to someone who asked about his racial background, he explained that he identifies as a Black Latino and his mother tongue is Spanish; but, however, other groups of people often identify him as an African American. His profession requires interactions with many ethnicities of people throughout the day and often as he stated "people are surprised that I speak Spanish and speak it so well and usually they ask if I learned the language as a part of my formal education." He emphasized that often through his exchanges with people, the general U.S. population is unaware that millions of Black Latinos/as exist in United States and around the world. He expressed his distain toward Spanish speaking news outlets and media platforms that he believed were contributing factors to the lack of exposure regarding Afro-Latinos/as visibility in the U.S. In addition, he believed that White Latinos/as who owned the Spanish speaking news and media outlets reinforced negative stereotypes of Black Latinos/as by only showing them in breaking news and stories that highlighted theft and crime.

When he was asked what it means to be an Afro-Latino/a in Washington, DC, he stated that (Afro-Latinos) have a unique language, food and cultural differences. Regardless, of his mother tongue, which is Spanish, Ed expressed his personal experiences with racism or racial discrimination in the United States which mostly had to do with being Black in comparison to being Latino. However, Ed voiced a distinction between being a Black Latino in the Washington, DC in comparison to the rest of the U.S. He believed that being an Afro-Latino has its benefits in the District where Black politics are prominent. He highlighted the facts that many African Americans and some Afro-Latinos/as are in positions of authority throughout the local and federal government in D.C. Whereas, in other regions of the United States, Afro-Latinos/as are nearly invisible in positions on local, state, and federal government level besides in south Florida, northern New Jersey, and the five boroughs that comprised New York City. He added, "even in these states Black Latinos/as do not have as much influence socially or politically as they do here in Washington DC."

Although, Ed realized that racism exist throughout the U.S. in many cultures, he stated that he experienced more discrimination because he is Black rather than Latino and often the discrimination comes from within the Latino community. He emphasized that often many people who migrate or have migrated from Latin America to the U.S. bring their colonial attitudes and beliefs with them. He expressed that Latinos/as of African descent throughout the Americas often experience subtle racism in their countries, however when white Latinos/as move to the U.S. they join ranks with American Whites for power and resources. Interestingly, he noted that race relations in the United States compared to race relations in his country of origin are not better or worse, "just different." He added that the devaluation of the person is the same and Brown and White Latinos/Latinas discriminate against him because that's the way they operate in their countries of origin and that discrimination happens to Afro-Latinos/as all the time and with more frequencies in the United States. He explained examples of when Afro-Latinos/as are subjected to unreasonable car searches by police officers, accusations of theft in retail and department stores, and constantly being mistaking for other black hotel guests or dinning patrons.

Ed was among many of the interviewees that believed skin color has a hierarchy in the social settings in the Latino community in the United States. He stated that "they get the jobs," meaning light-skin Latinos/as were offered "more opportunities" in matters of employment, social advancement and economic opportunities than their dark-skin counterparts. He stated that White or lighter-complexion Latinos/as migrate to the U.S. and advance at an increasing speed socially and economically in comparison to Black Latinos/as who were born in the U.S. and "did everything right" meaning received formal and advanced education to development a path to professional and personal growth and opportunities. He believes that employers are more likely to hire White or light-complexion Latinos/as over Black Latinos/as because they have more "European physical similarities." He also believed that this attitude spills over into the political arena where lighter-complexion Latino/a political representatives are viewed more favorable than dark-complexion Latino/a representatives. He added that "most representatives (Latinos/as) are lighter complexion and generally not Afro-Latinos/as." In addition, he highlighted his belief that most organizations and institutions that represent the Latino interest in the U.S. were governed by White and lighter-complexion Latinos/as and the efforts do not focus on Afro-Latino/a issues. In compassion, he believed that organizations and institutions that addressed Afro-Latino/a problems were headed by historically Black social and political institutions such as the National Urban League and the National Association for the Advancement of Colored People (NAACP). Also, Ed thought that lighter complexion is preferred over darker complexion in the United States, noting that "people prefer whiter things, i.e., skin and hair to look more European." He re-emphasized the Spanish speaking news outlets and media platforms that contribute to factors that highlight European cultures as the standard of a civilized society that Latin America can duplicate.

As some scholars such as Mark Hugo Lopez and Ana Gonzalez-Barrera have argued, when people think of the Latino vote or immigration, education, and language issues affecting Latinos, they generally have the larger groups in mind, i.e., Mexicans in the Southwest region and do not account for the ethnic distinctions or how the problems with Black Latinos/as are compounded and are afforded less attention. However, because Black achievement has been celebrated in the post-Civil Rights era in the United States, particularly in Washington, DC, many interviewees did not seem to view blackness as a liability compared to other parts of the United States. They proudly explained that Black people played integral roles in fighting for equality in society which gave them a sense of Black identity and pride. It was common for interviewees to celebrate their Black identities by talking about many movements led by African Americans they watched on television and other media outlets. The Civil Rights Movement was one with which most participants identified and reminded them to be proud of their African heritage, no matter in what part of the world they were born.

Ma, who was born in the Dominican Republic, migrated to the U.S. as a child, and grew up in Washington, DC, stated that in the District of Columbia, "African Americans take pride in their culture and being Black people" and added that "D.C. is the Mecca for Black intellectuals." He considered himself a Black Latino and believed that being Afro-Latino in Washington, DC is being Black from Latin America and that race-based consciousness is geared toward Dominican-Haitian identities compared to the United States identity of blackness. He stated that often when Dominicans from the island arrive to the U.S., they are surprised and often insulted to be considered "Black" by U.S. citizens. As he notes, in general being considered "Black" in Dominican Republic comes with a connotation of negativity usually associated with crime and violence. In addition, many Dominicans on the island identify as being "Indo" while most Haitians were considered "Black" and that identifying as Afro-Latino/a would normally be a combination of Indigenous and African heritage. He also stated that being Afro-Latino in his home country is based on skin color and physical characteristics. In addition, he noted that a person with darker skin will have less opportunities in the Dominican Republic and will not normally share the same spaces with light-skin people in society. In comparison to the United States, he believed that Latinos/as with lighter complexions are viewed more favorably in social settings than dark-skin Latinos/as or Afro-Latinos/as. However, he expressed that circumstances regarding social, economic, and political advancements were more complicated in the U.S. compared to his home country were White or lighter-completion Latinos/as general found easier access to resources, education, and property than their black counterparts. He believed that although lighter-complexion Latinos/as had an advantage over dark-skin or black

Latinos/as in the U.S., circumstantial matters such as foreign accents, cultural differences, and anti-Latino sentiments equally impacted the livelihoods of all Latinos/as.

Ma did not feel that Afro-Latinos/as have access to the same opportunities as other groups in the United States, noting the "lack of (Afro-Latinos/as) representatives at the local, state and federal levels in comparison to the White Latinos/as in the political arena. He added that he cannot mention any non-profit organization, embassies in DC, or organization/institutions that worked on issues that impacted the lives of the Afro-Latinos/as community in DC and the U.S. Although Ma believed that Afro-Latinos/as in DC have the same concerns in politics such as housing issues, undocumented Black immigrant issues and the lack of Black Latinos/as in leadership roles in major institutions, he also believed that one reason that contributes to the problems many Afro-Latinos/as face in Washington, DC is due to colorism in the community noting that "society amplifies Whiteness or Europeanness as being a model for my community to live by." He states that these ideas were imbedded during colonial rule and never challenged by most of the general Latino population because White and lighter-complexion Latinos/as benefited from the social, economic, and political norms. In addition, he thought that White Latino/a political representatives are viewed more favorably than Blacks stating the low numbers of Black Latino/a political candidates and elected officials on the local, state and federal levels. He believes one factor that is contributing to the low numbers of Afro-Latino/a elected officials is the "older generations" of Latino/a voters views of the typical Latino elected official. He notes that historically the typical Latino elected official was White or had European physical features, middle-aged and male. However, he highlights that the current political arena and representatives are becoming more diversified which includes Latinos/as from all ethnicities, ages and genders. Although he believes that the political arena for Latinos/as of all ethnicities is becoming more diverse, he was very careful to underline his belief that skin color comes to Latino/a voters' minds when electing a Latino/a political candidate in the United States as he referenced back to the lack of Afro-Latino/a political representatives. He noted that not only do Black Latino/a representatives experience different forms of racism with the White Latino community, the latter are racist toward non-Latino/a Black representatives as well, noting the derogatory language and racist remarks from the White Latino community directed toward Barack Obama and his wife, Michelle Obama. Lastly, he believed that "White Latinos/as are not interested in fighting against racism in the political arena because they benefit from whiteness."

While some respondents spoke of the contributions of Blacks in many areas of society such as music, religion, politics, and government, therefore demonstrating a consciousness of Black achievement, many other respondents acknowledged a sense of comradeship with other Blacks because of their physical appearance. For example, like most of the individuals interviewed for this project, Nel, who is a first-generation Afro-Latino, is often mistaken as a member of another Black ethnic group, particularly African American, based on his "skin color." He noted that being Afro-Latino in Washington, DC feels like possessing a dual identity, being both Black (African American) and Latino. He doesn't believe that he has to choose between one or the other because he is a Black person from a Latin American country. He stated that often skin-color played a role in his identity as well as other Afro-Latino/a identities because of the physical associations to other people his skin-color. He stressed that white and light-complexion Latinos/as have it easier when they are identified by their ethnicity from society because "they look Latino."

Like Nel, the majority of the people interviewed reported being mistaken for belonging to other groups, mostly African American, Dominican, Puerto Rican, African, or from an island in the Lesser Antilles. They are often thought to be from these countries, which share significant African heritage, making Afro-Latinos/as aware of their inclusion in a large African Diaspora. Like Nel, they looked at this connection as a matter of fact and were not offended when non-Black people associated them with other Black groups of people. However, Nel did not feel that Afro-Latinos/as have access to the same opportunities as other groups in the United States. He believed that their lack of social visibility prohibited them from equal access to advancements and resources. In addition, he expressed that often Afro-Latinos/as lack of visibility is due in part because they are meshed with African Americans, therefore losing their unique identity. Nevertheless, he believed that Afro-Latinos/as in DC have the same concerns and interests in politics such as access to jobs and education. Like Ed, he believes that the race relations in the United States compared to race relations in his home country is not better or worst but just different. He stated that skin color definitely is a factor in the Latino community and that lighter skin "represents intelligence" adding that light complexion is preferred over dark complexion in social settings in the United States. He highlighted events and social settings where Black or Afro-Latino/a people were treated as "second class or backup." He contributes the implications to a community that don't want to see Black Latinos/as "out of their places." Nel also thought that lighter-complexion Latino/a political representatives are viewed more favorably over dark-complexion Latinos/a representatives in the United States, adding that the (United States) definitely does not have a lot of Afro-Latinos/as in the political arena and that lighter-skin Latinos/as are higher in the political arena on a national stage. He notes that there really isn't an organization or institution that focus on Afro-Latino/a needs and that usually Black Latinos/as turn to African American institutions for social, economic, and political advancements. He further believed that skin color comes to Latino/a voters' minds "in some instances but not a defining factor," as people vote more on party lines and being Black would not be a determining factor for Latino/a voters. He stressed that Latino/a voters cast their ballots on matters that were most important to them and that the Latino vote was not a monolithic vote. He illustrated that a large majority of Latinos/as in south Florida vote more on the Republican party lines in contrast to a majority of Latinos/as in north New Jersey and New York City who vote more in line with the Democratic party. He believed that younger Latino/a voters were more likely to support and vote for political candidates based on their stances on issues over their skin-color. Nel remains optimistic that more Afro-Latinos/as will be elected into political office because younger voters are more energized in participating in political campaigns as well as their civil duty to vote.

Ro, who is a first-generation Afro-Latino in the United States, arrived in DC in the late 1970s. He illustrated how Black Latinos/as also draw on African American cultural symbols along with Caribbean ones to express pride in their blackness. He talked about how his experiences in the U.S. shaped this pride in being a Black Latino as follows: "I wasn't aware of the strong presence of Afro-Latinos in DC until I learned that in the 1930s and 1940s there were a lot of Afro-Cubans and Afro-Panamanians that were involved in fighting for civil rights alongside African Americans. I felt empowered after learning this history because there were so many black Latino/a people involved in civil rights whether it was in church, in sports or in politics."

And like Ro, Art, who was born in Panama and identified as Afro-Latino, shared a sense of Black pride and fond memories in Afro-Latino participation in civil affairs in Washington, DC when he said this: "I remember when we (Afro-Latinos/as) used to join demonstrations and protests with African Americans. We were not looked at as being Latino, just black like our brothers and sisters." However, some respondents encountered rejection from some by other non-Afro-Latinos/as and felt safer by bonding with African Americans. These sentiments even caused many of the participants to move and live in majority African American neighborhoods. Some interviewees expressed feeling more comfortable with or preferring to associate with African Americans than other Latinos/as even though they realized they were also not fully accepted by African Americans. And when asked about their political stance in regards to seeing more Afro-Latino/a political leaders in Washington, DC most of the respondents viewed the electability of an Afro-Latino/a in the District of Columbia as a positive step.

For instance, Rob, a 36-year-old first generation self-identified Afro-Latino from South America, believed that Afro-Latinos/as will serve all Latinos and not just one ethnicity of the Latino community, stating that "Yes, we (Afro-Latinos/as) are capable of doing a great job in serving the community." He believed that skin-color plays a role when electing a political candidate into office as he highlights most Latinos in political office on the local, state, and federal levels as well as administrators that lead organizations or institutions are white or light-completion. Although he stated there are Afro-Latinos/as in positions of influence in DC, systematic and institutional racism has prevented many of them from being elected into political offices in DC as well as across the United States. He emphasized that light complexion is preferred over dark complexion in social settings. And, light complexion Latinos/as political representatives are viewed more favorable over dark completion Latino/a representatives in the United States, pointing to Senator Rafael Edward Cruz (R-Texas) and Senator Marco Rubio (R-FL) as examples. He expressed that the road to political office for white or light-completion Latinos/as was less difficult because "race relations in the United States are worst compared with race relations in his home country" noting that white or light-complexion Latinos/as leverage off their whiteness to achieve social, economic, and political success.

Rob states that mobility for Afro-Latinos/as was more possible in his home country than the U.S. because more mechanisms are in play for the advancement of all Latinos/as. Whereas Afro-Latinos/as do not have access to the same opportunities as other groups in the United States because they (Afro-Latinos/as) are invisible in both the Latino and African American communities. Moreover, he believed that Afro-Latinos/as in Washington, DC do not have the same concerns and interests in politics because "they are more interested in getting money and they don't have time for politics." He also believed that most organizations and institutions do not represent the best interests of the Afro-Latino community; however, he noted that the DC Afro-Latino Caucus and Senator Bernie Sanders (D-Vermont) represent his political interests and those of the Afro-Latino community in Washington, DC politics. Rob further stated that the best way for Afro-Latinos/as to achieve their political goals in Washington, DC is to organize and get Afro-Latinos/as that live in the neighboring states of DC such as Maryland and Virginia to start a movement to empower Afro-Latinos/as in order to seek visibility in their community as well as win seats for political offices.

Ros, a first-generation Afro-Latina who described herself as a Spanish-speaking Black woman, also believed that the Latino community is ready for more Afro-Latino/a political leaders in Washington, DC. She stated that the Afro-Latino community wants "everyone to unite." She believed that the most important issues for Afro-Latinos/as in Washington, DC is having a sense of wholeness and creating a community. She said that "Afro-Latinos/as in Washington, DC have the same concerns and interests in politics, "but everybody is different." Like Rob, she also believed that DC Afro-Latino Caucus represents the best interests of the Afro-Latino community in Washington, DC. She didn't believe that most organizations and institutions represented the best interests of the Afro-Latino community, however she believed the Organization of American States (OAS) did work to some extent to address issues in the Afro-Latino community. Furthermore, Ros believed that political leaders such as Mayor Muriel Browser (D-DC), Senator Elizabeth Warren (D-Massachusetts) and Former First Lady Michell Obama represent the interest of her and her community because they include people from all walks of life on their platforms.

Like many other interviewees, Ros felt that skin color had a hierarchy in the social settings in the Latino community in the United States. She stated that race relations in the United States were more complicated compared to race relations in her home country where in her country "people are all mixed with multiple nationalities" noting the U.S. has a more rigid racial identification structure. Nonetheless, she also believed that Afro-Latino men were treated more respectably than Afro-Latina women because "they (Afro-Latino men) are considered more desirable in dating circles." Also, Ros noted that light complexion was preferred over dark complexion in social settings in the United States and that "dark-skin (Latinos/as) generally had to compromise themselves." Furthermore, she stated that dark-skin Afro-Latinas received the worst treatment in the Latino community compared to their counterparts who had lighter skin complexions; and, when it came to the matter of skin complexion and political representation, she believed that light-complexed Latinos/as are viewed more favorably than dark complexion Latinos/as because "they (non-Afro-Latinos/as) fit the norm of what Latinos look like." She believed that skin color came to Latino/a voters' minds when electing a Latino/a political candidate in the United States, and like many other interviewees, she expressed her disappointment of having to hear racism directed at Black Latino/a political candidates in the United States and believed their path to being elected to political office as a more challenging one due in part to racism. However, like Nel, she believes that many younger voters in DC cast their ballots for political candidates based on their principles and morals they share with them rather than the candidate's physical appearance.

Marie, a 55-year-old, first-generation Dominican who has lived in Washington, DC for over 25 years expressed the same sentiments as many other interviewees regarding the social and racial factors that influence the electability of light and dark-skin self-identified Afro-Latinos/as running for political office in Washington, DC. Like Ros, she believed that skin color comes to Latino/a voters' minds when electing a Latino/a political candidate in the United States., noting that "if they (Latinos/as) had to choose between a White Latino/a political candidate or someone else, they would choose the White Latino/a." But like Ros and Nel, she believed that many younger voters in DC cast their ballots for political candidates based on their principles and morals they share with them rather than the candidate's physical appearance.

She did not believe that any current political leaders, organization or institution represents the interests of the Afro-Latino community in Washington, DC. In addition, she believed that skin color had a hierarchy in the social settings in the Latino community in the United States, stating that "White Latinos/as are in higher social settings than the rest of us (Afro-Latinos/as)." She expressed that "lighter-complexion Latinas were considered more desirable in social settings because the closer you look European, the more attractive people think you are." She believed that race relations in the United States were worse than race-relations in her country because, as she noted, "people are constantly being reminded of their race in this country and that race questions are everywhere, whether it's on your job application, applying for a credit card, or buying a car."

Although Marie thought that the light-complexion and White Latinos/as are more at a social advantage than dark-complexion or Afro-Latinos/as, she also believed that they had access to the same opportunities as other groups in the U.S., adding that "the opportunities for Afro-Latinos/as are greater in the U.S., especially in the Metro (DC, Maryland, and Virginia) area, because there are so many opportunities for us (Afro-Latinos/as)." Also, she believed that Afro-Latinos/as in DC have the same concerns and interests in politics, i.e., education, jobs, representation and that the most important issue for Afro-Latinos/as in Washington, DC is the older generation's failing to embrace other ethnicities in the Latino community. She felt that many Afro-Latinos/as intentionally do not want to interact and merge with other members of the Latino community, "which hampers our (Afro-Latino/a) growth." Although she did not believe there are any political representatives that represent the interests of Afro-Latinos/as in Washington, DC, she did think that Mayor Muriel Bowser's Office of Latino Affairs could be the best way for Afro-Latinos/as to achieve their political goals in the District of Columbia and that the office should provide more information to the community about Afro-Latino/a agendas.

Many of the respondents saw the negative role skin color played in their countries of origin, but Jun, a first-generation self-identified Afro-Latino from the Dominican Republic, pointed out that skin color played an even more negatively significant role in the social settings in the United States stating that "Dark skin people in the DR (Dominican Republic) are everywhere but light-skin Latinos/as think they are better. Dark-skin is considered ugly. We all live together, but they don't hate each other. But living here (U.S.), people are judged by the color of their skin and people hate you for that."

And, like many of the interviewees, Jun believed that skin color had a hierarchy in social settings in the Latino community in the United States and noted that "black skin is not at the bottom but under the bottom." He felt that light complexion is preferred over dark complexion in social settings in the

United States and that light-complexion Latino/a political representatives or "definitely" viewed more favorably over dark-complexion Latino/a representatives in the United States. He adds that dark-skin or Afro-Latinos/as political candidates must go above and beyond to prove their worthiness for office even if they have more education and experience over their competitor, especially if they are white or light-skinned. Also, he believed that skin color came to Latinos/as voters' minds when electing a Latino/a political candidate in the United States. Interestingly, he believes that we (Afro-Latinos/as) are ready to take the role as an elected officials in DC but the people (Afro-Latinos/as) are not ready noting "they will not support Afro-Latino/a candidates like that."

ANALYSIS OF THE FINDINGS AND CHAPTER SUMMARY

In sum, the participants interviewed as illustrated in Table 3.1 demonstrated their experiences with what it meant to be "Afro-Latino/a" in the U.S. society, more specifically in Washington, DC. Their experiences reflected traditional United States racial binaries and recent political and demographic realities in the United States. Their everyday encounters confirmed that the negative ideologies about what it means to be Black or Latino/a in this society have real effects on the daily lives of people who have those identities as well as their electability into political offices. Some Afro-Latinos/as felt that they were not accepted as real "Blacks" among African Americans and they found that many United States Latinos/as could not associate a Latino identity with blackness.

Also, many Black Latinos/as felt rejected by many White Latinos/as in their community. As noted in this chapter, the United States dependence on a "one drop rule," which defines anyone with African ancestry as "Black," is not congruent with many people from the Caribbean racial descriptions that are typically used for an array of color and phenotypic descriptors based on both physical and social characteristics (Newby and Dowling, 2007). For example, in the Dominican Republic, many people use the category "Black" to refer to Haitians as noted by one of the interviewees for this study named Man. Also, many Dominicans tend to avoid the categorization Black (Negro) and instead use several skin color categories that are also dependent on an individual's social class. Thus, when many Dominicans of African ancestry arrive in the United States, they often refuse the label "Black," as it does not fit with their understanding of blackness (Newby and Dowling, 2007).

However, as this research shows, many Afro-Latinos/as take pride in being Black in the United States, particularly in DC, especially when there is a social and political incentive. As Candelario notes in Washington, DC,

Table 3.1: Interview Participants

Source: Self-generated by the Author Using Information from the Interviews

Name	Afro-Latino/a?	Age	Gender	Foreign born?	Neighborhood	Political Affiliation	Education	Skin color?
Nel	Yes	30	Male	Yes	Mix	Democrat	Bachelor's degree	Medium Complexion
Man	Yes	33	Male	Yes	AA & White	Democrat	Bachelor's degree	Medium Complexion
Ed	Yes	50	Male	Yes	AA	Democrat	Master's Degree	Medium Complexion
Ed. C	Yes	40	Male	Yes	White	Democrat	Master's Degree	Dark Complexion
Art	Yes	60	Male	Yes	AA	Democrat	Some College	Medium Complexion
Ro	Yes	65	Male	No	AA	Democrat	Some College	Dark Complexion
Rob	Yes	36	Male	Yes	AA & White	Democrat	Master's Degree	Medium Complexion
Jun	Yes	34	Male	Yes	AA	Independent	Some College	Dark Complexion
Jen	Yes	39	Female	No	White	Democrat	Bachelor's degree	Light Complexion
Ang	Yes	32	Female	No	Mix	Non-party Affiliation	Bachelor's degree	Dark Complexion
Marie	Yes	55	Female	Yes	Mix	Democrat	Some College	Dark Complexion
Ros	Yes	26	Female	Yes	AA	Democrat	Bachelor's degree	Dark Complexion
Ro. M	Yes	32	Female	No	AA	Democrat	Bachelor's degree	Medium Complexion

there was and continues to be an incentive for Black self-identification. In the District of Columbia, African Americans are a numerical majority, wield increasing political power, hold the vast majority of government posts and jobs, and occupy a diversity of socioeconomic statuses. For example, just outside DC, Maryland's Prince Georges County has the largest percentage of affluent Blacks in the country. The class stratification of the African American community in Washington, DC also serves as an incentive to assimilate into a Black racial identity (Candelario, 2001).

And, although there is an incentive for Afro-Latinos/as to assimilate with other Black groups in DC, many of the interviewees highlighted a strong sense of self-determination to be recognized and represented by other Afro-Latinos/as in the Latino community. However, social considerations influence racial classifications in the continuum model (Roth, 2012). According to Roth, in the Latino community, greater socioeconomic status, prestige, or social networks can lead to a "lighter classification." Also, pigmentocracy is used to rank groups and individuals based on their skin color. She further recognizes that "color has real consequences for social outcomes in the Caribbean just as it does in the United States." In addition, she notes that social status and color are closely related (Roth, 2012).

In the post-Obama era, many Afro-Latinos/as in the DC have a strong sense of the political implications associated with their skin color and the possibilities of being elected or electing an Afro-Latino/a into political office. For many Afro-Latinos/as, the road ahead for equality is only through gaining access to political representation. As discussed in qualitative analysis of the interviews, most participants believed that social and racial factors influence the electability of a self-identified Afro-Latino/a running for political office in Washington, DC, noting that light-complexion or White Latino/as are viewed more favorably than Afro-Latino/a political candidates. Therefore, the first Hypothesis of this study, H1: Social/racial factors influence the electability of light and dark-skin self-identified Afro-Latinos/as running for political office in Washington, DC, is acceptable.

Chapter 4

Pathways to Political Office

The discussion here, similar to what was done in chapter 4, pertains to the results dealing with the second major research question of the study: How do social/racial factors influence the pathway to political office for self-identified Afro-Latinos/as in Washington, DC? This chapter is divided into four sections. The first section provides a theoretical discussion on representing and theories of representation; the second section provides a theoretical discussion on typology of representation; the third section discusses the qualitative results; the fourth section provides an analysis of the findings and determines the tenability of the hypothesis of the preceding research question.

The interviewees' comments regarding this question were in response to the discourse on colorism as it impacts the ability of Afro-Latinos/as electability to achieve public office. Interviewees were asked to identify the following factors and explain their response to the question. The five principal factors mentioned in the interview were (1) ethnicity, (2) skin-color, (3) campaign finance, (4) voter turnout, and (5) non-support from other Latino/a representatives, all of which influence the pathway to political office for self-identified Afro-Latinos/as in Washington, DC. Before discussing the results, I will begin with theoretical discussions of *representing* and *typology of representation* to serve as theoretical backdrops for the results that follow. These aspects will add to the brief denotations on the concepts of formalistic representation, symbolic representation, substantive representation and descriptive representation in Chapter 3 of this book. The rationale for doing this is that the major reason political candidates seek pathways to political office is to *represent* their constituents in the political system.

REPRESENTING AND THEORIES OF REPRESENTATION

Representing as employed in this book means serving in a political system by delegated authority. Thus, a *representative* is a person who acts for or on behalf of other people in the decision-making process of that political system. Accordingly, *representation* is a result of the conditions that allow for some members of a society to act for that society as a whole. We glean from Roderick Bell and David Edwards that a distinction can be made between "external" and "internal" representation when they state the following:

> *External representation* indicates the political society seen from without. We might know very little about the internal organization of a country—the People's Republic of China, for a god example—and yet find that country effectively and undeniably represented as an existing viable political system . . . *Internal representation* is the political society experienced from within. The articulated institutions of a society—president, king, parliament—and the relations among its members constitute the common framework within which reality is perceived by individuals in the society. (Bell and Edwards, 1974, pp. 5–6)

Therefore, the articulation of any democratic society, as is the case of the United States, naturally involves many political struggles among those citizens who seek to represent their fellows. In order to get a good understanding of these political struggles, it is imperative to discuss the notion of *representing* vis-à-vis the following two major aspects: (1) theories of representation and (2) types of representation. The first aspect is addressed in the rest of this section and the second aspect is broached in the subsequent section for the sake of lucidity.

In their interrogations of the theories of representation, Herbert R. Winter and Thomas J. Bellows (1985) and Robert L. Cord et al. (1985) describe three classical and four contemporary theories that have been tendered to explicate the phenomenon. According to these scholars, these theories cover perspectives that span from the allocation of all popular authority to the sovereign, to rule by the "general will" with direct popular participation or of indirect representation. The subsequent discussion is based to a great extent on the treatises of the aforementioned scholars, albeit the perspectives of other scholars on the issues are included where they are relevant.

Beginning with the classical theories of representation, first, the *Hobbesian Theory of Representation* proffered by Thomas Hobbes (1588–1679) is a response to why people form governments because without such an instrument, nobody could be protected from attack. In order to perfect themselves, people long ago formed governments, gave up their political independence, and formed a "social contract" that authorized the sovereign to make laws that would protect everyone equally. According to Hobbes, government was established on the "consent of the governed," with the caveat that once authority is given to the sovereign it cannot be taken back. Even if the sovereign were to become tyrannical, the people cannot trade him/her for someone else. Taking into consideration his observation of the English civil wars, Hobbes argued that anarchy (the state of nature), where everyone is free to do as s/he pleases, is worse than even the most despotic ruler (Winter and Bellows, 1985; Cord et al., 1985).

Second, the *Lockean Theory of Representation* postulated by John Locke (1632–1784) modified Hobbes' postulation by proposing that rulers must be accountable to the governed. Locke argued that the "social contract" binds the government and the people to a set of responsibilities; thus, the people are to obey the government only if it honors its responsibilities to protect them. Should the government violate the trust, then the people have the right to replace it (Cord et al., 1985).

And, third, the *Rousseaunian Theory of Representation* posited by Jean-Jacques Rousseau (1712–1778) differs from the theories of Hobbes and Locke. Rousseau avowed that representation goes concurrently with inequality and loss of freedom. He nonetheless perceived humans to be intelligent, rational human beings and are quite capable of making their own decisions. Therefore, for Rousseau, the ideal is a "city-state" in which everyone can play a role in the deliberative assemblies of government. Thus, for him, representatives are to transmit decisions, and nothing more (Winter and Bellows, 1985; Cord et al., 1985).

Together, the Hobbesian, Lockean and Rousseaunian Theories of Representation constitute a series of postulates dealing with issues ranging from the allocation of all popular authority to the sovereign to rule by the "general will" with direct popular participation. Given that these philosophers were writing about events occurring from the 1500s to the 1700s, a profitable question to be asked here is the following: What theories exist about contemporary representation.

As it pertains to the contemporary theories of representation, as mentioned earlier, four of them have been proposed and will be described in the subsequent paragraphs. It is important to note here that in the examinations of contemporary representation theories, two issues appear to reoccur. One of these issues deals with the obligation representatives have to the people who elect them. The other issue is about how much control voters should have over the representatives they elect. These issues are adequately addressed in the contemporary theories of representation.

First, the *Symbolic Theory of Representation* deals with a context where the head of state is the "symbol" of that state, as s/he represents the people by "standing for" them. For example, in the United Kingdom, Queen Elizabeth II is said to "stand for" the people, and her lifestyle reflects the traditional power and glory of the country. Nonetheless, very few people today would be content to elect a representative to office solely on the basis that s/he "symbolizes" the national or local character. Instead, most voters are more concerned about how a representative will act on their behalf once in office (Cord et al., 1985).

Second, the *Constituent Theory of Representation* deals with the type of action of speaking or acting on behalf of people by a representative who is elected from a particular constituency and whose responsibility is to vote for all bills that will help that constituency, even though some of these bills may work to the disadvantage of the rest of the country. The issue that arises relating to this form of representation is whether or not representatives should vote their conscience, even when it means going against the wishes of their constituents (Cord et al., 1985).

In response to the preceding dilemma, Edmund Burke (1729–1797) proposed that whereas a representative must act on the behalf of his/her constituents, s/he is, however, not bound to act the way they would wish at all times. His rationale for this position is that a representative ought to represent the entire country, not just his/her constituency. Burke himself was a member of the British parliament and felt that he represented the entire British Empire, not just his district of Bristol. As Burke argues, this idea does not violate the principle of representative government because if the constituents do not like the way their representative acts, they can vote him/her out of office at the subsequent election (Winter and Bellows, 1985; Cord et al., 1985).

The counter perspective to that of Burke is that a representative is elected to act for his/her constituents and she/he must act as they want him/her to act, even if it means going against his/her better judgment. The major difficulty with this theory of representation is the challenge of finding out what constituents actually want so that the representative can carry out their wishes. For instance, in the United States, the average congressperson represents nearly half a million people, and the likelihood that she/he will speak to or receive mail from even five percent of that number is slim, even on major issues. Compounding the problem is the fact that there is always a wide span of public opinion on any issue (Cord et al., 1985).

Third, the *Correspondence Theory of Representation* is an outgrowth of the fact that even if a representative were able to act as the voice of his/her constituency, she/he could easily be accused of being unrepresentative on other grounds. This is due to the fact that most representatives are not at all representative in reflecting the social makeup of their constituencies. For the most part, representatives are middle-or upper-class professionals (often lawyers), overwhelmingly males, commonly older than most of their constituents, and much better educated than them as well. For instance, in the state legislatures of the United States, White Anglo-Saxon Protestants (WASPs) are dominant in the legislative bodies (Cord et al., 1985).

According to some observers, the solution to this problem hinges upon having representatives in government who correspond to the characteristics of the general public Thus, in the case of the United States, for example, since 53 percent of the population is female, these observes say that its legislative bodies should comprise 53 percent female as well. They add that the proposed government should also be composed of African Americans, Latinos/Latinas, Native/first Americans, Jews, Roman Catholics, etc. in proportion to their populations (Cord et al., 1985).

Fourth, and finally, the *Functional Theory of Representation* is an attempt to resolve the inevitable dilemma of the correspondence approach to representation. At the heart of the functional idea of representation is that the legislature should be structured around the key socioeconomic interests in the country: i.e., agriculture, the arts and sciences, industry, organized labor, etc. rather than geographical districts. Each of these socioeconomic interests would then be assigned seats according to its relative size and importance to the economy, and the people would then vote not as individuals, but as businesspeople, farmers, laborers, etc. (Cord et al., 1985).

The Irish Seanad (Senate) employs the functional approach of representation. Of the 60 members of that body, 11 are chosen by the prime minister and six by the universities; the remaining 43 are elected by the national legislature and county borough councils from lists of candidates generated by five vocational panels. These panels are constituted according to occupational categories whose choices represent agricultural, commercial, cultural, educational, industrial and labor interests. Nonetheless, the Irish Seanad is partly a ceremonial upper house with very little power (Cord et al., 1985).

Also, we are apprised by Charles Anderson, Fred Mehden and Crawford Young (1967) that the functional approach to representation has been utilized as the most widespread and effective formula for coming to terms with diversity in a number of countries. The formula has been called "balanced ticket" in ethnically conscious areas of the United States, especially New York and New England, or what has been referred to as "ethnic Arithmetic" in West Africa. In such cases, efforts are consciously made to distribute the visible leadership functions within the state in some rough proportion to the strength and self-consciousness of the primary cultural groups within the polity (Anderson et al., 1967).

In addition, Anderson and his coauthors cite Lebanon as probably the most glaring case of functional representation whereby the president is, by institutionalized tradition, a Maronite Christian; the prime minster is a Sunni Muslim; and the chairman of the parliament is a Shi'ite Muslim. For many years before the bloody and protracted civil war, the formula made it possible for primary groups to have a psychic assurance that their communal interests were being defended, and that there would be no risk of the state being converted into an engine of hegemony of one cultural group over the others (Anderson et al., 1967).

TYPOLOGY OF REPRESENTATION

In this section, I employ the same approach utilized by Charles F. Andrain (1983) to compare the structural dimensions of state power, instead of describe types of representation according to formal government institutions: i.e., cabinet, courts, law, parliament, presidency, etc. Accordingly, I base my general descriptions on the common structural dimensions that mirror interactions among the central state organs, lower government agencies, and social groups. Concomitantly, I identify five types of representation. They are discussed independently in the ensuing paragraphs for clarity.

First, *Monopolistic Representation* is the type whereby a powerful representative dominates the decision-making process, denying lower government agencies and social groups the right to make policies. A monopolistic representative utilizes the military and police as agents of physical coercion to wield crucial control. She/he tends to prevail at the early stage of a country's development (Andrain, 1983).

As Andrain apprises us, in Europe between 1600 and 1800, "absolute monarchs" ruled states like France, Prussian Germany, Spain and Russia. In France, for instance, Louis XIV proclaimed "L'État, c'est Moi" (in English, "I am the state"). Also noted by Andrain is that similarly, after African territories won political independence from their European colonizers during the late 1950s and early 1960s, monopolistic rule became widespread across the continent. Even though colonial rule had destroyed the traditional monarchies, new presidential monarchies emerged, led by nationalist politicians or military officials (Andrain, 1983).

Second, *Centralized Representation* exists when representatives in the national government gain dominance over representatives of local political units such as municipal governments, provincial administrations, town councils, and village assemblies. The centralized approach makes it possible for those representatives in the national government to maintain the territorial integrity of the country. Also, we are reminded by Winter and Bellows (1985) that centralized representation existed in the Soviet Union and the Eastern European bloc. In the Soviet Union, for example, although the constitution vested al powers in the elected "Supreme Soviet," effective power was in the hands of the Communist Party which controlled both the government and the nomination processes for local and Supreme Soviets. This type of representation can be seen in a number of countries including Cuba and the People's Republic of China.

Third, *Coordinated Representation* refers to a state of affairs where representatives of a single agency formally orchestrate the functional activities of government. As Andrain points out, in many Western societies, for instance, the monarch originally claimed to exercise "sovereignty": i.e., absolute legal right to make final decisions that are binding on everyone in the society. The monarch and his/her royal bureaucracy coordinated central government activities. When the monarch lost his/her power, the dominant political party, parliament, or the president assumed the sovereign authority formerly exercised by the monarch (Andrain, 1983).

Also, Stig Hadenius (1985) informs us that in Sweden, for instance, the instrument of government that remained in force until 1974 had been adopted in 1809. The instrument stipulated that the country was a monarchy in which the King "alone" would govern the society. Members of the Swedish Riksdag (Parliament) nonetheless had the power to levy taxes and shared lawmaking power with the King. The Riksdag was divided into four estates: (1) nobility, (2) clergy, (3) burghers, and (4) peasants. These estates reflected the economic and social structure of a preindustrial society. Having outlived its usefulness, the Riksdag was abolished in 1865. The nobility no longer enjoyed the influence that had once clearly justified an estate of its own in the Riksdag, while many of the newer "aristocrats" of trade and industry did not have representation in any estate. The four-estate Riksdag was therefore replaced with the bicameral Riksdag that better reflected the changing power structure of Sweden (Hadenius, 1985).

Fourth, *Specialized Representation* exists in places where representatives become both differentiated (i.e., specialized) and independent. Andrain tells us that ancient government forms such as the one that existed in the Athenian city-state made no clear distinction between representatives in the public sphere and those in the private sphere. The activities of these representatives were neither differentiated nor independent from those of other social groups such as leading families, the church, and economic associations. The emergence of the nation-state saw political activities being performed by more specialized representatives in legislatures, executives, administrative bodies, and courts. These representatives also sought to gain functional autonomy from powerful primordial, economic and religious groups (Andrain, 1983).

Fifth, and finally, *Comprehensive Representation* can be found especially in industrialized countries in which representatives exercise a wide scope of power, thereby performing a complete variety of activities that include the construction of economic infrastructure, system maintenance, and the provision of social services. As Andrain recounts, when the modern nation-state was birthed during the 15th Century, representatives concentrated on system maintenance: i.e., the preservation of the territorial integrity of the fragile nation-state. Accordingly, representatives devoted most of their time on public policies that dealt with defense, foreign affairs, internal order, the raising of revenues by levying taxes, and printing currency (Andrain, 1983).

Andrain adds that at the beginning of the 19th Century, the construction of an economic infrastructure assumed greater importance as a distinctive activity of representatives. Consequently, policies designed by these representatives stimulated the development of public works such as canals, railways, and roads. The era also saw postal and telegraph services spread widely. In addition, representatives provided subsidies to promote agriculture, commerce, and industry (Andrain, 1983).

Furthermore, Andrain points out that during the 20th Century, and especially after World War I, the growing popularity of democratic values, the rising strength of socialist movements, the industrialization process, and the severe effects of the two world wars prompted representatives to design public policies that allocated social services to individuals. Nonetheless, as Andrain also notes, the advancement of industrialization made individuals less self-sufficient. As a result, the growing specialization of labor, interdependence, and social personality triggered demands for representatives to enact public policies that would meet individual needs. Thus, since World War II, representatives in every modern democracy have spent an increasing share of public revenues on basic human needs programs, which include education, food, healthcare, and shelter. By enacting policies that increase these programs, the scope of power of representatives has also increased (Andrain, 1983).

In sum, what is evident from the analyses in the preceding two sections is that the *action structure* (i.e., the phenomenon which directs people's attention to the occurrence of voting and representing and to the decision procedures through which these actions emerge) is critical for understanding why political candidates seek pathways to political office. The acts of voting and representing in modern democracies occur in linear sequences; they are not randomly ordered; and, there is a pattern and predictability to their occurrences. Also, acts of voting and representing are situated in a polity, such that what counts as a particular action is strongly constrained by what action precedes, what action is intended, what action is intended to follow, and what action actually does follow. Consequently, action structures are critical in fulfilling the ritual constraints of political behavior which constitute the interpersonal requirements of a democratic society.

In addition, it is not surprising that every modern democracy emphasizes voting and representing as significant aspects of political participation. Voting and representing are perceived to be major sources of power for citizens, and they do in fact allow them to remove corrupt, incompetent, or insensitive officials from office and influence issues. Nonetheless, voting has severe limitations as a means of exercising power. This is because, to commence with, the span of candidates from which voters can choose is limited due to the importance of political parties. Next, since the purposive behavior of all political parties is to win elections, normally, only candidates endorsed by the major parties have greater chances of winning political offices. Accordingly, Maurice Deverger (1954) posits that many groups are not effectively represented. Also, the limited choice of political candidates is reinforced by the high cost of political campaigns. Only politicians who are wealthy enough to help finance their own campaigns or who are able to attract large financial contributions from supporters can mount effective campaigns. Such politicians are most likely not representative of the general public, and powerful contributors expect favors once the candidates whose campaigns they financed win political offices.

Finally, representatives are contacted to act as intermediaries to channel interests primarily because most citizens believe that a representative's voice is more effective than their own. Most people perceive representatives to be the overseers of the governmental establishment. This is mostly because the activities of the administrative agents are guided by the rules established by the representatives. A very accessible representative is therefore frequently enlisted by the people to channel their interests to other elected representatives.

QUALITATIVE RESULTS

Amongst the various responses for this study, many social/racial factors were noted to influence the pathway to political office for self-identified Afro-Latinos/as in Washington, DC. For instance, Rob who is a self-identified Afro-Latino highlighted many factors such as racism in the Latino community, lack of financial contributions, and the dearth of support from the broader Latino community to influence the pathway to political office for self-identified Afro-Latinos/as in Washington, DC. He also noted that non-support from other Latino/a representatives was a contributing factor and that, ultimately, skin-color was the major influencing factor because "Latinos/as are very concerned about appearance," adding that "the more you look European, the more society accepts you."

Man, who is also a self-identified Afro-Latino, agreed with Rob, noting that racism and non-support from other Latino/a representatives influence the pathway to political office for self-identified Afro-Latinos/as in Washington, DC, stating that "White Latino politicians have shown us (Afro-Latinos/as) with deeds that they don't care about our issues." He also noted the lack of support non-Afro-Latino/a representatives shown toward Afro-Latino/a candidates running for political office. In addition, he stated that Latino institutions catered to White Latinos/as which left many Afro-Latinos/as behind in society. He further expressed the lack of investment from the White Latino/a representatives, noting that "Afro-Latinos/as have experienced the most hardship in areas of immigration, economics, housing, education, health and political office." Moreover, he believed that White Latino/a representatives "intentionally neglected Afro-Latino voices," making it impossible to believe that they (White Latino/a representatives) would ever support an Afro-Latino/a running for political office. He highlights that most organizations and institutions that represent the Latino interest in the U.S. are managed by white or non-black Latinos as such as the National Association of Latino Elected and Appointed Officials (NALEO), National Hispanic Institute (NHI), United States Hispanic Chamber of Commerce, and the League of United Latin American Citizens (LULAC). Moreover, he expressed that these same organizations and institutions that are managed by mostly white Latinos/as align with American whites to leverage their own self-interest.

Man also mentioned ethnicity as a factor that influences the pathway to political office for self-identified Afro-Latinos/as in Washington, DC, saying that "Because without a clear understanding of our (Afro-Latino/a) ethnicity, the non-Afro-Latino/a community has added to more inequality in our (Afro-Latino/a) community in terms of resources." Also, Man added another interesting factor that influence the pathway to political office for self-identified Afro-Latinos/as in Washington, DC by stating that "it's sad because when we (Afro-Latinos/as) have political or institutional power, we (African descendants) favor the whole community, not just African descendants' folks." He pointed out the desire of many Black Latino/a candidates and representatives to represent the entire Latino community in comparison to their White counterparts.

Nevertheless, not all participants viewed the factors that influenced the pathway to political office for self-identified Afro-Latinos/as in Washington, DC in the same way. For example, Ed C., who identified as an Afro-Latino, has lived in the District of Columbia for over ten years after emigrating from South America, believed that Afro-Latino/a candidates running for political offices had the same opportunities as their non-Afro-Latino/a counterparts and that Afro-Latino/a access to public office was based on their creditability. He stated that Afro-Latino/a candidates had a greater advantage to public office because of the overwhelming representation of the Black community in Washington, DC. He also believed that "location mattered" and that Afro-Latinos/as could leverage their electability into political office in DC by galvanizing the African American and Afro-Latino/a votes whereas White Latinos didn't have the same power. As he acknowledged that the race relations in the United States were a factor that influences the pathway to electability for Afro-Latinos/as into political offices, he also strongly believed that ultimately economic factors such as campaign contributions and wealthy donorship solidified which candidates will win their election. He believed that racism has been institutionalized and that there wasn't "clear direction" for Afro-Latinos/as to address the matter while on the campaign trail. He emphasized that "if more Afro-Latinos/as focus on fundraising while running for office and less on racism and other distractions, it might be less difficult for them to win." He also believed that if Afro-Latinos/as candidates had access to more public resources and advanced their "get out to vote" efforts, the possibility of being elected would be more obtainable.

Also, Ed C. believed that many White non-Latino/a residents were in favor of electing an Afro-Latino/a candidate into political office which "stacked the cards" in their favor in comparison to White Latinos/as in DC. However, Ed C. was very aware of the influence skin-color played among Latino/a candidates in the political arena, acknowledging that light-complexion Latino/a political representatives are viewed more favorably than dark-complexion Latinos/as "because they are the majority." He added that in the Latino community, White Latinos/as make up the majority in many elected public offices such as trade unions, judgeship, sectorial and appointed positions. Furthermore, he stated that light-skin Latino/a candidates were given preference over Afro-Latino/a candidates because they resembled the appearance of previous elected officials and they do not want to accept the change now.

Like Ed. C, Nel also echoed the same sentiment that "location mattered," stating that social/racial factors that influence the pathway to political office for self-identified Afro-Latinos/as in Washington, DC and that circumstance changed "depending on where the Afro-Latino/a candidate was running for office." He believed that the electoral experience differed based on where the location of the Afro-Latino/a candidate submitted his/her bid to run for office, noting that "it's different for an Afro-Latino/a running in Iowa than it is in New York or Pennsylvania." He cites the fact that more Afro-Latinos/as and the other Black people from the Diaspora make up large majorities of the constituent bases in cities in states such as New York and Pennsylvania. Like other interviewees, he believed that skin color influences the pathway to political office for self-identified Afro-Latinos/as in Washington, DC, stating that "You definitely don't see a lot of Afro-Latinos/as in the political arena." He mentioned that lighter-complexion and White Latino/a political representation was highest on a local and national scale and that Afro-Latinos/as had little to no opportunity as their lighter-complexion and White Latino counterparts in the political arena.

In addition, Nel believed that skin color came to the Latino/a voters' minds when electing a Latino/a political candidate in DC, but not always, emphasizing that "in some instances the issue comes to the voters' minds, but it's not a defining factor." He also noted that "People vote more on party lines and that being Black would not determine a voter's decision." He believed that skin color would always play a factor regarding the challenges Afro-Latinos/as face while pursuing political office in Washington, DC; however, voter turnout is also essential. He stated that more Afro-Latino/a participation in local elections was vital for Afro-Latinos/as to achieve their political goals in DC as well as across the U.S.

Ros, a mid-twenties Dominican living in Washington, DC, was among the most outspoken interviewees for this project. She stated that ethnicity and skin-color influence the pathway to political office for self-identified Afro-Latinos/as in Washington, DC; however, the Latino community was ready for more Afro-Latino/a political leaders in the District of Columbia "because they (Afro-Latinos/as) want everyone in the Latino community to unite." Nevertheless, she also stated that factors such as campaign finance, voter turn-out, and non-support from other Latino/a representatives decrease the chances for Afro-Latinos/as to gain political office in DC.

Ros also expressed that skin color played a significant role in the electability for Afro-Latinos/as citing that light-complexion Latino/a political representatives were viewed more favorably than dark-complexion Latino/a representatives because they (light-complexion and White Latinos/as) fit the norm of what "Latinos/as" look like and that "they would never vote for someone who looked like me (dark-complexion)." Furthermore, she expressed her disappointment regarding the lack of support from other ethnicities, i.e., White Latinos/as representatives, who she felt did not support Afro-Latino/a candidates in the past while they were on the campaign trail in Washington, DC. She further mentioned that the Latino/a representatives on the national political landscape and the Latino community "don't have anyone who looks like us (Afro-Latino/a representatives) to begin with." In addition, she believed that skin color came to Latino/a voters' minds when electing a Latino/a political candidate in Washington, DC because she has heard racist remarks aimed at African Americans and other Black politicians in the United States and abroad.

Jen highlighted the generational gap between younger and older voters in the Latino community, stating that younger voters were more likely to vote for an Afro-Latino/a candidate in DC compared to the older voters "because they were accustomed to seeing non-Afro-Latino/a representatives." She expressed her aspirations in the young generation of Latino/a voters who she believed were more "colorblind" in terms of voting for an Afro-Latino/a candidate for political office in Washington, DC. However, she explained that many young Latino/a voters in other parts of the United States needed to progress socially and racially with the rest of the country: i.e., many Cuban voters in south Florida.

Jen also noted that the Black Lives Matter movement helped highlight social and racial inequality in the United States that not only impact African Americans but Afro-Latinos/as too. She believed that the Black Lives Matter movement helped to challenge the stereotypes in the Latino community and provided more leverage for Afro-Latino/a candidates seeking political offices in Washington, DC and other parts of the United States. Moreover, she believed that the younger Afro-Latino/a community has more influence in political matters due in part to their "support from the liberal White community," stating that "younger White people are more vocal about Black issues today than their parents were in the past." She added that she sees the support of a lot of white people at Afro-Latino/a events in DC. Jen also believed that the Black Lives Matter movement along with the support from the African American and White community, could help more Afro-Latino/a candidates gain access to political office in Washington, DC, and that skin color is becoming less of a factor on the campaign trail because "more medium-Brown and dark-skin Afro-Latinos/as are getting access to powerful positions in the political arena."

However, Marie believed that skin color came to a Latino/a voter's mind when electing a Latino/a political candidate in DC because "if they (non-Afro-Latino/a) voters had a choice, they would elect a candidate who is White and not Afro-Latino/a." Like Jen, she believed that the electability for Afro-Latinos/as in DC was an exception to the rest of the country besides New York and New Jersey because "a lot of African Americans were willing to support an Afro-Latino/a candidate for political office in Washington DC." She explained that the Latino community was ready for more Afro-Latino/a political leaders in Washington, DC because "there are group of communities, i.e., African American, Caribbean and Central and South Americans that are demanding so." Furthermore, Marie believed that governmental institutions are demanding for Afro-Latinos/as be included in the decision-making process. She processed that skin color has always been a factor that influences the pathway to political office for self-identified Afro-Latinos/as in Washington, DC, but "the influence becomes less of a factor each decade with the Latino/a voters."

Like most of the interviewees, Ed believed that skin color was a factor that influenced the pathway to political office for self-identified Afro-Latinos/as; however, he also emphasized more specifically that "skin color and hair texture" were very important physical characteristics that contributed to the social acceptance of persons in the Latino community when he stated that "You (Afro-Latino/a) must have a look that is esthetically pleasing to other Latinos/Hispanics" and that "colorism" is an issue which we (Afro-Latinos/as) were all familiar with." These sentiments were also expressed by other interviewees who believed that not only did Afro-Latino/a political candidates' skin color influenced their pathway to political office in DC, but their physical attributes such as hair texture and facial features did so as well.

Also, Ed stated that active support from Afro-Latinos/as for the candidate was critical, adding that non-Afro-Latinos/as would generally not support an Afro-Latino/a candidate that does not have the active support of the Afro-Latino community. Furthermore, he expressed that "If the Afro-Latino/a candidate made a legitimate effort to engage the African American community, the likelihood of support for him/her would increase in an election." He in addition believed that light-complexion Latino/a political representatives were viewed more favorably than dark-complexion Latino/a representatives in DC, and in the United States in general because "most Latino/a representatives were light-skin and mostly not Afro-Latino/a."

ANALYSIS OF THE FINDINGS AND CHAPTER SUMMARY

All of the participants interviewed for this study expressed their beliefs regarding factors that influence the pathway to political office for self-identified Afro-Latinos/as in Washington, DC. Although there were many factors discussed during the interview such as campaign finance and voter-turn out, most participants believed that skin-color and non-support from non-Afro-Latino/a representatives and the Latino community at large were most influential. The interviewees' beliefs and experiences reflected the perspective of Garcia (1994) who also believed that the American understanding of race and ethnicity is strongly related to skin color and serves as an external influence on group identification. He notes that in Latino communities, the development of pan-ethnic grouping and identity becomes a means to expand the group, its scope, and national visibility. Thus, the outgrowth of "Hispanicity" or Latino-ness represents a strategic decision among activists to enlarge the community and, potentially, its political capital and resource base. Also, Wendy D. Roth stated in her book, Race Migrations: Latinos and the Cultural Transformation of Race that "color is a racialized physical attribute that is often used in Latin America in ways similar to how North Americans use race to stratify and structure society and to value particular racialized bodies over others" (2012, p. 58).

Identity politics has long played a significant role in the outcome of elections in the United States. For instance, during the Jim Crow era, many African Americans in the South saw electing Black candidates into political offices as a method to express national grievances and provide a platform to advance their social and economic agenda. Although the "one drop" rule was in effect, lighter-skin African Americans had a greater chance of being elected into public office at any level. For instance, out of the ten Black officials elected into the Senate, eight of them passed the "brown bag test" or were of mixed races such as Hiram Rhodes Revels whose mother was of Scottish descent, Blanche Bruce whose father was a White Virginia planter, former U.S. President Barack Obama whose mother was of English descent, and Kamala Harris whose mother is a Tamil Indian. However, the notion of identity and ethnicity or the "one drop rule" doesn't classify or categorize members of the Latino community as does the United States racial structure. Many scholars point out that when minority candidates are on the ballot and campaigning for political office, race and ethnicity often become central to the coverage of the campaign (Gay, 2001). In some cases, the candidates themselves provide racial cues to prospective voters for perceived electoral benefits (JoneReeves, 1994; Ttaugott, Price & Czilli, 1993; Is, 1987; Jones & Clemons, 1993). The media may also highlight race in these elections, regardless of the cues provided by the candidates themselves. In either case, voters are provided with racial or ethnic cues that can impact election outcomes and promote a sense of political commonality or identity among minority voters.

Nonetheless, Latinos/as who identify as Black racially are less likely to perceive a sense of political commonality with other Latinos/as. The role of race for this segment of the Latino/a population may lead Afro-Latinos/as to perceive greater levels of perceived commonality with African Americans than with other Latinos/as (Logan, 2003; Nicholson, Pantoja & Segura, 2005). This perception may also be partially due to Afro-Latinos/as being subjected to discrimination in Latin America and the United States by lighter-skin Latinos/as (Wade, 1997; Andrews, 2004; Peña, Sidanius, and Sawyer, 2004; Logan, 2003; Nicholson, Pantoja and Segura, 2005), which can decrease perceptions of political commonality. Sanchez and Morin (2011) demonstrate in their research that panethnic-based representation leads to positive political outcomes as well, decreasing political alienation among Latinos/as. They reveal that descriptive representation has normative value beyond substantive representation for the Latino population. More specifically, their results suggest that the rise in descriptive representation has an influence on not only how Afro-Latinos/as view government and politics, but also how they feel about their relationship with other Latinos/as.

Jennifer L. Hochschild and Vesla Weaver (2007) noted the complicated relationship between skin-color and electability into political office. In their study, they reveal that African American elected officials were disproportionately light-skin and that people with lighter skin were overrepresented among elected political elites. Their research is a survey of a nationally representative sample of Blacks that varied in terms of skin tone, platforms, and names of candidates in a hypothetical election for Senate to provide evidence for the impact of skin color on candidate favorability. The results show that the light-skin Black candidate prevailed over the darker opponent by 18 percentage points, a larger margin than any other treatment group received. The respondents also rated the light-skin Black candidate as being more intelligent, more experienced, and more trustworthy than the dark-skin opponent.

Therefore, colorism (pigmentocracy) operates in the political realm in much the same way that it does in the socioeconomic realm. In addition, some political scientists have shown that individuals' social, economic and cultural characteristics link to their political views (Weaver, 2008). As discussed in the qualitative analysis of the interviews, most participants believed that factors such as ethnicity and skin color influenced the pathway to political office for self-identified Afro-Latino/a in Washington, DC, noting that light-complexion or White Latinos/as are viewed more favorably than Afro-Latino/a political candidates. Some interviewees also mentioned campaign finance, voter turnout, and non-support from other Latino/a representatives as factors that influence the pathway to political office for self-identified Afro-Latinos/as in Washington, DC. Therefore, the second Hypothesis of this study, H2: Social/racial factors influence the pathway to political for self-identified Afro-Latinos/as in Washington, DC, is tenable.

Chapter 5

Summary, Conclusions, and Policy Recommendations

In this final chapter, the discussion is divided into three sections. Section one is a summary of the major points in the previous chapters; section two draws some conclusions made possible by the findings in those chapters; and, section three offers some policy recommendations.

SUMMARY

This research sought to analyze the political underrepresentation of Afro-Latinos/as in the District of Columbia. The main objective of this book is to identify presumed factors that influenced the social/racial attitudes of Afro-Latino/a voters and political representatives, and how pigmentocracy played a role in the Afro-Latino/a community. Also, the study sought to understand the low representation in political offices from the Afro-Latino/a community in Washington, DC. As demonstrated in this study, many theories on Afro-Latino/a identity have been proffered by scholars such as Anani Dzidzienyo, Pierre-Michel Fontaine and Peter Wade; but, yet, many questions still remain. Also, scholars such as Silvio Torres Saillant, Clara E. Rodriguez, Wendy D. Roth, Stephen E. Cornell and Douglas Hartmann have helped to shed light on ethnicity and pigmentocracy in the Latino community, but still more questions also remain. Moreover, John C. Wahlke and Hanna F. Pitkin have presented different points of views regarding representation, as the notion of representation may be regarded as an effort by elected or other public officials to build more inclusive, deliberative and engaged relationships with the public (Orr & McAteer, 2004).

Given that the major objective of the study was to examine the supposed impact ethnicity and pigmentocracy had on the electability of Black and darker-skin Latinos/as in Washington, DC, the following major research questions emerged: Q1: What social/racial factors influence the electability of light-skin and dark-skin self-identified Afro-Latinos/as running for political office in Washington, DC? Q2: How do social/racial factors influence the pathway to political office for self-identified Afro-Latinos/as in Washington, DC? In light of the preceding questions, the following hypotheses were therefore suggested for scientific testing: H1: Social/racial factors influence the electability of light-skin and dark-skin self-identified Afro-Latinos/as running for political office in Washington, DC. H2: These factors influence the pathway to political office for self-identified Afro-Latinos/as. From these hypotheses and the research questions, the central thesis that undergirded this study was therefore stated as follows: Social/racial factors influence the pathway to political office for self-identified Afro-Latinos/as in Washington, DC.

The conceptual framework that guided this study was quite straightforward. First, it was proposed that the discourse on colorism as it impacts the ability of Afro-Latinos/as to achieve public office hinges upon three principal attributes: (1) the characterization of being Afro-Latino/a (CBAL) in the U.S., specifically in DC; (2) the politics of ethnicity versus nationalism (PEVN); and (3) pigmentocracy's impact on the opportunity and electability of Latinos/as of African descent (PIOELAD) in political offices in Washington, DC. As defined earlier, CBAL in the United States refers to the distinctive description of a Black Hispanic or Afro-Hispanic (Spanish: Afrohispano) who is racially Black and is from Latin America and/or speaks the Spanish language natively; PEVN refers to the fact or state of belonging to a social group that has a common national or cultural tradition and the exclusion and inclusion of a group just as racism does; and PIOELAD connotes a discriminatory practice based on skin color and is a form of prejudice or discrimination in which human beings are treated differently based on the social meanings attached to skin color.

CBAL, PEVN, and PIOELAD are suggested to jointly influence the ability of Afro-Latinos/as to achieve public office. The framework represents a continuing sequence of attributes in a circular flow. Each attribute had the same level of importance. The framework was therefore conceptual in that as Chava Frankfort Nachmias and David Nachmias point out, in a conceptual framework, which constitutes "the third level of theory, descriptive categories were systematically placed in a broad structure of explicit propositions, statements of relationships between two or more empirical properties, to be accepted or rejected" (Frankfort-Nachmias and Nachmias, 1996, p. 38). Studying this topic was important for many reasons; but for this work, the most important ones were categorized under three broad heading, namely (1) practice, (2) literature, and (3) theory. In terms of practice, this work sought to be relevant to politicians, administrators, academicians, researchers, students and voters as a guide in their own work and studies. As it pertains to literature, this study sought to add to the body of works in Political Science and in Afro-Latino/a studies. And as for theory, this research explained the viewpoints, made connections, and predictions required in my research.

The introduction discussed the theoretical framework and research methodology. The philosophical model that served as the theoretical framework for this study is Racial Democracy Theory, which generally refers to certain patterns of race relations within a system of government by the whole population or all the eligible members of a state, typically through elected representatives.

A scholarly work is scientific because of its research methods, which can be defined as the blueprints that guide a researcher in the various stages of the research process. In this chapter, the research methodology employed in the study was explained. Primarily, the research was qualitative, as I employed an interpretive and naturalistic approach to examine the subject matter. Qualitative research is primarily exploratory research. This type of research methodology was best used to gain an understanding of underlying reasons, opinions, and motivations. Also, it provided insights into the problem and helped me to develop ideas for potential quantitative research.

A combination of the Descriptive and the Explanator Case Study methods was used to analyze the data collected this study. The Descriptive Case Study method helped me to describe the characteristics of the population. The Explanatory Case Study method was used to focus primarily on describing the nature of the demographic segment, while emphasizing the why factor. A case study, while narrow in scope, provided an opportunity to fully understand the dynamics operating in Washington, DC in terms of Afro-Latinos/as pursuing and achieving public office. For this study, both primary and secondary data were utilized for this research. Primary data were collected from self-identified Afro-Latino/a interviewees. Secondary data were retrieved from books, journals, magazines, newspapers, and reliable online sources on the subject.

Chapter 1 discussed the term *pigmentocracy* as well as provided an overview of the ethnicities of Latin America. In this chapter, historical content regarding ethnic compositions in Washington, DC as well as the Latino/a community was provided to the reader. Also, this chapter provided background on Washington, DC and the Afro-Latino/a political officials. In addition, there was a discussion on colorism in the Afro-Latino/a community.

Chapter 2 entailed a review of the competing perspectives that pertained to the topic under investigation and comprised of journal articles and books that captured the nexus among Black self-identity, pigmentocracy, and political representation. This chapter examined the works of scholars in relation to the electability of dark-skin self-identified Afro-Latinos/as into political office and explored concepts such as formalistic representation, symbolic representation, substantive representation and descriptive representation, and how these notions apply in the case of the Afro-Latino/a voting community. There was a brief theoretical discussion on identity and the competing perspectives was organized in a synchronic approach based on the three themes from the conceptual framework: (1) Afro-Latino/a Identity in the Americas and the United States; (2) Views Regarding Ethnicity and Pigmentocracy in the Latino Community; and (3) Descriptive Representation and Electability of Dark-skin Self-identified Afro-Latinos/as to Political Office. Also, there was a discussion that covered the limitations in the competing perspectives.

Chapter 3 dealt with the first major research question of the study. To restate the question: What social/racial factors influence the electability of light-skin and dark-skin self-identified Afro-Latinos/as running for political office in Washington, DC? This chapter was divided into three sections. The first section provided a conceptual discussion on ethnicity; the second section presented the qualitative results; the third section analyzed the findings and determined the validity of the hypothesis of the major research question investigated in that chapter. As the results indicated, social/racial factors influence the electability of light-skin and dark-skin self-identified Afro-Latinos/as running for political office in Washington, DC.

Chapter 4 dealt with the second major research question of the study: How do social/racial factors influence the pathway to political office for self-identified Afro-Latinos/as in Washington, DC? This chapter was divided into four sections. The first section provided a theoretical discussion on representing and theories of representing; the second section provided a theoretical discussion on typology or representation; the third section entailed a discussion of the qualitative results; the fourth section analyzed and determined the validity of the hypothesis of the major research question probed in that chapter.

This chapter also evaluated the pathway to political office for self-identified Afro-Latinos/as in Washington, DC. It concluded that the social/racial factors that influence the pathway to political for self-identified Afro-Latinos/as in Washington, DC included skin-color, ethnicity, campaign finance, voter turnout, and non-support from other Latino/a representatives.

CONCLUSIONS

Many conclusions can be drawn based on the findings in the preceding chapters. First, the conceptual framework that guided this study was very useful for investigating the topic. The lack of Afro-Latino/a representatives in Washington, DC was driven by social/racial factors such as skin-color that influence their pathway to political office. These objectives have been considered to be fundamentally sound. It is equally important to note that the framework can be used by experts, academicians, researchers and students as a good reference point for theory building in Political Science and Afro-Latino/a Studies.

Second, the combination of the Descriptive and Explanatory Case Study methods proved the be quite useful. The approach made it possible to delineate what has happened in regard to Afro-Latinos/as seeking political office in Washington, DC and why it happened.

Third, it is evident from the review of the relevant literature that previous works on Afro-Latino/a identity in the other Americas and the United States, views regarding ethnicity and pigmentocracy in the Latino community, descriptive representation and electability of dark-skin self-identified Afro-Latinos/as to political office offered plenty of information that was constructive for getting the basic understanding of this subject. Moreover, it was equally obvious that this work is grounded both theoretically and methodologically. In essence, this study will assist academicians, researchers, and students in Political Science and Afro-Latino/a Studies by providing them new empirical information to evaluate the social/racial issues that impact Afro-Latinos/as.

Fourth, this work reviewed a range of competing theories and approaches for identity, ethnicity, skin-color and political representation. It also explored the historical and intellectual evolution in scholarly thinking about how and why Afro-Latinos/as are elected or not elected into political office. As illustrated by Mansbridge, in practice, descriptive representation attempts to improve inequitable social conditions by providing historically marginalized groups such as Afro-Latinos/as the opportunities to become political elites. In so doing, proponents assert that descriptive representation safeguards the interests of the disadvantaged. Addressing inequitable political representation, theoretical debates focus on the tenability and philosophy of descriptive representation as a governance solution, especially in light of the current state of disadvantaged group representation (Mansbridge, 1999). This study therefore addresses both an ideal and a reality, with the ideal being the governance solution and the reality being the degree to which legislative bodies represent the demographics and experiences of the citizenry.

Fifth, the findings on the first and second major research questions affirmed that social/racial factors influence the electability of light-skin and dark-skin self-identified Afro-Latinos/as running for political office in Washington, DC differently. Also, social/racial factors influence the pathway to political office for self-identified Afro-Latinos/as in Washington, DC. These findings implicate that Afro-Latino/a political candidates are less likely to be elected into public office compared to their White Latino/a counterparts in Washington, DC. In addition, these findings show that social/racial factors such as skin-color and ethnicity influence the electability of light-skin and dark-skin self-identified Afro-Latinos/as running for political office in Washington, DC. Lastly, these finding show that campaign finance, voter turn-out, and non-support from other Latino/a representatives also influence the electability of light-skin and dark-skin self-identified Afro-Latinos/as running for political office in Washington, DC.

POLICY RECOMMENDATIONS

As the world observed the 2020 United States Presidential election, many milestones were made to change the course of the political history across the country. One milestone that was the election of the first woman of color as Vice-President, Kalama Harris, and another was the election of Georgia's Senate Democrats Jon Ossoff and Raphael Warnock. These milestones played a significant role in the course of the 2020 political strata, which historically and mainly reserved for White, Christian, and male domination. The Latino community in Washington, DC needs a new transformation and departure from the racial/social factors that have influenced the electability of Afro-Latinos/as in political offices in DC. The District of Columbia needs a new voter's blueprint, such as the Stacey Abrams blueprint, to get young, disadvantaged, and "people of color" voters registered and increase voter turn-out. This blueprint is known for changing the presidential and senate elections in Georgia from Red to Blue. In addition, this resulted in the election of two Democratic Senators as well as numerous local and state Democratic candidates in the state of Georgia. Abrams started the New Georgia Project and Fair Fight Project to register current voters and new voters. This project sought to register disadvantaged voters, young voters, first-time voters, and "people of color." The same principles should be applied to voters in Washington, DC. The objective here is to achieve self-reliance and voter enthusiasm in the Latino community for Afro-Latino/a political candidates and, as my research has demonstrated young Latino/a voters are less likely to allow social/racial factors to influence their vote for an Afro-Latino/a candidate compared to older Latinos/as.

Based on the findings of this study, a couple of policy recommendations are suggested: First, all residents of the District of Columbia should be encouraged and supported to register to vote if they meet the standard requirements for registration. In addition, DC residents could be automatically registered to vote for the next election cycle if they meet the requirements for voter registration.

Lastly, "dark money" circulates through many campaigns for political candidates in DC; therefore, monetary caps on campaign contributions should be employed to ensure fair and equal elections. The Latino community and particularly, the Afro-Latino community in DC, currently lacks the financial independence needed to run successful campaigns compared to their White Latino/a and non-Latino/a counterparts.

Bibliography

Abizadeh, A. (2001). "Ethnicity, race, and a possible humanity." *World Order* 33(1): 23–34.
Abramo, L., Cecchini, S., Espíndola, E., Maldonado, C., Rodrigo Martinez, V., Milosavljevic, V., Palma, A., Sunkel, G., Tromben,V., Trucco, D., Ullmann, H., and Rangel, M. (2016). "Economic Commission for Latin America and the Caribbean (ECLAC)." *The Social Inequality Matrix in Latin America.* (See page 23).
ACS Demographic and Housing Estimates. (2013). "American Community Survey 1-Year Estimates." US Census Bureau. 2013. Archived from the original on January 2, 2016
Ahmed, Nizam. (2017). *Women in Governing Institutions in South Asia; Parliament, Civil Service and Local Government.* University of Chittagong, Bangladesh. Palgrave MacMillan.
Alford. N. S. (2018, October 4). "More Latinas Are Choosing to Identify as Afro-Latina." *The Oprah Magazine.*
Anderson, C. W., Mehden, F. R. von der and Yooung, C. (1967). *Issues of Political Development.* Englewood Cliffs, NJ: Prentice-Hall, Inc.
Andrain, C. F. (1983). *Foundations of Comparative Politics: A Policy Perspective.* Monterey, CA: Brroks/Cole Publishing Co.
Andrews, G. R. (2008). "Afro-Latin America by the Numbers." *ReVista Cambridge17*(2): 38–40.
Appiah, A. and Gates, H.L. (2005). *Africana.* Oxford University Press, UK.
Austin, Sharon and Middleton, Richard. (2015). *Whither A Coalition? Afro Latino Consciousness, Participations of Blacks.*
Ballantine, J. H., Roberts, K. A. and Korgen, K. O. (2019). *One Social World.* Thousand Oaks, CA: Pine Forge Press.
Bangura, Abdual Karim, Thomas, A., and Hopwood, J. (2014). "A Comprehensive Introduction to Research Methods." Volume 2. *Qualitative Methods.* San Diego, CA: Cognella Press.
Barreto, M. (2007). "!Si Se Puede! Latino Candidates and the Mobilization of Latino Voters." *American Political Science Review*, Vol. 101, No. 3.

Bell, R. A. and Edwards, D. E. (1974). *American Government: The Facts Reorganized.* Morristown, NJ: General Learning Press.

Brennan, Jonathan. (2002). *Introduction. Mixed race literature.* Stanford, CA: Stanford University Press.

Britannica Online Encyclopedia. "South America: Postindependence Overseas Immigrants." Retrieved February 10, 2008.

Brown, M. E., ed. (1996). *The International Dimension of Internal Conflict.* Cambridge, MA: Massachusetts Institute of Technology Press.

Candelario, G. E. (2001). "Black Behind the Ears" and Up Front Too? Dominicans in The Black Mosaic." *The Public Historian*, 23(4), 55–72.

Características Étnico-raciais da População." (PDF). biblioteca.ibge.gov.br. 24 February 2021.

Cheadle, N., Osorio, M., Torres, L., Young, R., Barrios, N. B., Potvin, C., . . . & Den Tandt, C. (2007). *Relocating Identities in Latin American Cultures* (No. 2). University of Calgary Press.

Clemons, M.L. and Jones, C. E. "African American Legislative Politics in Virginia." *Journal of Black Studies*, Volume 30 Issue 6: 744–76. Sage Publications.

Cord, R. L., Medeiros, J. A., Jones, W. S. and Roskin, M. G. (1985). *Political Science.* 2nd ed. Englewood Cliffs, NJ: Prentice-Hall, Inc.

Cornell, S., & Hartmann, D. (2007). *Ethnicity and Race: Making Identities in a Changing World.* Sage Publications, Ltd.

Countrystudies.us. "Venezuela—ETHNIC GROUPS." October 14, 2015. https://familypedia.fandom.com/wiki/Afro-Latin_Americans#Venezuela.

Cuevas, A. G., Dawson, B. A., & Williams, D. R. (2016). "Race and Skin Color in Latino Health: An Analytic Review." *American Journal of Public Health.* 106(12), 2131–2136. https://doi.org/10.2105/AJPH.2016.303452.

Current Elected Officials in DC. D.C. Board of Elections and Ethics. https://www.dcboe.org/Elections/Past-Elected-Officials. Retrieved January 11, 2012

D.C. Board of Election, 2016 Election Results, dcboe.org/election_results/2016-General-Election

De Genova, Nick. (2005). *Working the Boundaries: Race, Space and "Illegality" in Mexican Chicago.* Durham, NC: Duke University Press.

DeSipio, Louis, (2006). *Hispanics and the Future of America.* Washington, DC: National Academies Press (US).

Diaz, Joseph, (2005). "School Attachment Among Latino Youth in Rural Minnesota." *Hispanic Journal of Behavioral Sciences*, Vol. 27, No. 3, August 2005.

Duany, J. (1998). "Reconstructing Racial Identity: Ethnicity, Color, and Class among Dominicans in the United States and Puerto Rico." *Latin American Perspectives*, 25(3), 147–172.

Duverger, M. (1954). *Political Party.* New York, NY: John Wiley and Sons.

Economic Commission for Latin America and the Caribbean, 2017a and 2017c.

Erikson, E. H. (1950). *Childhood and Society.* New York, NY: Norton.

Erikson, E. H. (1959a). "Identity and the life cycle: Selected papers by Erik H. Erikson." *Psychological Issues*, Monograph 1. New York, NY: International University Press.

Erikson, E. H. (1959b). "The problem of ego identity." *Psychological Issues*, Monograph 1. New York, NY: International University Press.

Erickson, E. H. (1968). *Identity: Youth and Crisis*. New York, NY: Norton.

Erikson, E. H. (1974). *Dimensions of a New Identity*. New York, NY: Norton.

Fernandes, Florestan. (1969). *The Negro in Brazilian Society*. New York: Columbia University Press.

Fontaine, P. M. (1980). Research in the Political Economy of Afro-Latin America. *Latin American Research Review*, *15*(2), 111–141.

Frankfort-Nachmias, C. and Nachmias, D. (1996). *Research Methods in the Social Sciences*. New York, NY: St. Martin's Press.

Freedman, J. L. (1982). *Introductory Psychology*. 2nd ed. Boston, MA: Addison-Wesley Publishing.

Gale, Thomson. (2006). *Encyclopedia of African American Culture and History*, 2006.

Garcia, J. A., & Sanchez, G. R. (2021). *Latino Politics in America: Community, Culture, and Interests*. Rowman & Littlefield.

Garcia, Nathalie and Thurber, Maria. (2021): Latinx Studies: Library of Congress Resources. *Afro-Latinx Bibliography*. https://guides.loc.gov/latinx-studies/afro-latinx-bibliography.

Garcia, Ruben J. (1995). "Critical Race Theory and Proposition 187: The Racial Politics of Immigration Law." *Scholarly Works*. 662. https://scholars.law.unlv.edu/facpub/662.

Garcés Montes, Elizabeth. (2007). *Relocating Identities in Latin American Cultures*. Calgary: University of Calgary.

Gates, Jr., Henry Louis. *Black in Latin America*. New York: New York UP, 2011. (See page 2).

Gates, Jr., Henry Louis, and McKay Y. Nellie. (1997). *The Norton Anthology African American Literature*. New York, N.Y.: W. W. Norton & Company, Inc. p. 2665.

Gates. Jr., Henry L. (2011). "What It Means To Be 'Black In Latin America." - NPR, Fresh Air, July 27.

Gay, Claudine. (2001). *The Effects of Minority Districts and Minority Representation*. San Francisco, CA: Public Policy Institute of California. (See page 40, third paragraph).

Ginsberg, S. D. and Orlofsky, J. L. (1981). "Ego identity status; ego development; and ego locus of control in college women." *Journal of Youth and Adolescence* 10:297–307.

Gosin, Monika. (2009). *(Re) Framing the Nation: the Afro-Cuban Challenge to Black and Latino Struggles for American Identity*. University of California-San Diego.

Hadenius, S. (1985). *Swedish Politics During the 20th Century*. Stockholm, Sweden: The Swedish Institute.

Hanchard Michael. (1994). *Orpheus and Power: The Movimento Negro of Rio de Janeiro and São Paulo, Brazil, 1945–1988*. Princeton: Princeton University Press.

Harren, V. A. (1976). An overview of Tiedeman's theory of career decision making and summary of related. Unpublished manuscript, Southern Illinois University,

Carbondale. Retrieved on March 28, 2022 from https://files.eric.ed.gov/fulltext/ED123364.pdf
Harris, Trudier. (2022). "Pigmentocracy." Freedom's Story, TeacherServe©. National Humanities Center.
Hernandez, Tanya. (2003). *Too Black to Be Latino/a: Blackness and Blacks as Foreigners in Latino Studies.* 1. 152–159. 10. 1057/palgrave.lst.8600011.
Hernández, Tanya Katerí. *Colorism and the Law in Latin America—Global Perspectives on Colorism.* Conference Remarks, 14 WASH. U. GLOBAL STUD. L. REV. 683 (2015). https://openscholarship.wustl.edu/law_globalstudies/vol14/iss4/12.
Hero, R. (1992). *Latinos and the US Political System: Two-Tiered Pluralism.* Philadelphia: Temple University Press.
Higgins, S. M. (2007). Afro-Latinos: An Annotated Guide for Collection Building. *Reference & User Services Quarterly*, 47(1), 10–15.
Hochschild, J. L., & Weaver, V. (2007). The Skin Color Paradox and the American Racial Order. *Social Forces*, 86(2), 643–670. 10.1353/sof.2008
Huddy, L. (2001). From social to political identity: A critical examination of social identity theory. *Political Psychology* 22(1):127–156.
Ipl.org.stateyknowledge: Facts about the United States & The District of Columbia, U.S. Census Bureau.
Jackson, J., Hutchings, V., Brown, R., and Wong, C. (2004). *National Politics Study.* Ann Arbor, MI: Inter-university Consortium for Political and Social Research.
Johnson, Ollie A. III (2012). "Race, Politics, and Afro-Latin Americans." In Kingstone, Peter; Yashar, Deborah J. (eds.). *Routledge Handbook of Latin American Politics.* London: Routledge. p. 302.
Jones, L. K. and Chenery, M. F. (1980). Multiple subtypes among vocationally undecided college students: A model and assessment instrument. *Journal of Counseling Psychology* 27:469–477.
Juenke, E.G., & Preuhs, R.R. (2012). Irreplaceable Legislators? Rethinking Minority Representatives in the New Century. *American Journal of Political Science,* 56(3), 705–715.
Laó-Montes, A. (2005). Afro-latinidades and the diasporic imaginary. *Iberoamericana (2001-),* 5(17), 117–130.
Latorre, S. (2012). Afro-Latino/a Identities: Challenges, History, and Perspectives. *Anthurium: A Caribbean Studies Journal,* 9(1), 5.
Lizcano Fernandez, Francisco. (May–August, 2005). "Ethnic Composition of the Three Cultural Areas of the American Continent at the Beginning of the XXI Century Convergence." *Journal of Social Sciences,* Vol. 12, No. 38, Autonomous University of the State of Mexico Toluca, Mexico. (See pp. 185–232).
López, Gustavo, & Gonzalez-Barrera, Anna. (2016). Afro-Latino: A deeply rooted identity among US Hispanics. *Pew Research Center.*
Lowe, Lisa. (1996). *Immigrant acts: On Asian American cultural politics.* Durham, NC: Duke University Press.

Maio, Marcos. (2001). "UNESCO and the study of Race Relations in Brazil: Regional or National Issue?" *Latin American Research Review.* Vol. 36, Issue 2. (See pp. 118–136).

Mansbridge, J. (1999). Should Blacks Represent Blacks and Women Represent Women? A Contingent" Yes." *The Journal of Politics, 61*(3), 628–657.

Marcia, J. E. (1980). Identity and adolescence. In Adelson, J. (ed.). *Handbook of Adolescent Psychology.* New York, NY: Wiley.

Marx, A. (1997). *Making Race and Nation: A Comparison of South Africa, the United States, and Brazil.* Cambridge University Press.

Metraux, A. (1950). United Nations Economic and Security Council statement by experts on problems with race. *American Anthropologist* 53(1):142–145.

Metropolitan Policy Program at Brookings: State of Metropolitan America on the Front Lines of Demographic Transformation, 2010.

Miller, A. L. and Tiedeman, D. V. (1972). Decision making for the 70s: The cubing of the Tiedeman paradigm and its application in current education. *Focus on Guidance* 5(1):1–14.

Mochkofsky, Graciela. (2020)."Who Are You Calling Latinx?" *The New Yorker.* September 5.

Moore, Joan W. and Pachon, H. (1985). *Hispanics in the United States.* Englewood Cliffs, NJ: Prentice Hall.

Nachmias, Chava-Frankfort, David Nachmias, and Jack DeWaard. (2014). *Research Methods in the Social Sciences.* 7th ed. New York, NY: Worth Publishers/Palgrave Macmillan.

Newby, C. A., & Dowling, J. A. (2007). Black and Hispanic: The Racial Identification of Afro-Cuban Immigrants in the Southwest. *Sociological Perspectives, 50*(3), 343–366.

Newman, B. M. and Newman, P. R. (2017). *Development through Life: A Psychological Approach.* 13th ed. Homewood, IL: The Dorsey Press.

Orr, K. & McAteer, M. (2004). "The Modernisation of Local Decision Making: Public Participation and Scottish Local Government." *Local Government Studies,* 30 (2), 131–155.

Nicholson, S. P., Pantoja, A. D., & Segura, G. M. (2005). Race Matters: Latino Racial Identities and Political Beliefs. Presentation at the Annual Meeting of the American Political Science Association, Washington, DC.

Pachon, H. & DeSipio, L. (1992). Latino Elected Officials in the 1990s. *American Political Science Association.* Vol. 25, No. 2, p. 212–217.

Pantoja, A. D., & Segura, G. M. (2003). Does ethnicity matter? Descriptive representation in legislatures and political alienation among Latinos. *Social Science Quarterly, 84*(2), 441–460.

Pennock, J. & Chapman, J. (1968). *Nomos X: Representation.* New York: Artherton Press.

Petroni, F. A. (1971). Teen-age interracial dating. *Transaction* 8:54–59.

Pew Research Center, Fact Tank, News in the Numbers. (2019). *Hispanics with darker skin are more likely to experience discrimination than those with lighter skin.*

Pew Research Center. (2021). *Majority of Latinos Say Skin Color Impacts Opportunity in America and Shapes Daily Life.* Luis Noe-Bustamante, Ana Gonzalez-Barrera, Khadijah Edwards, Lauren Mora and Mark Hugo Lopez.

Pitkin, Hanna F. (1967). *The Concept of Representation.* Berkeley: University of California Press.

QuickFacts. (July 1, 2017). "District of Columbia." U.S. Census Bureau.

"Racial Democracy in Brazil." In *Encyclopedia of African-American Culture and History.* Encyclopedia.com.

Rivera, M. Q. (2006). From Trigueñita to Afroâ Puerto Rican: Intersections of the Racialized, Gendered, and Sexualized Body in Puerto Rico and the US Mainland. *Meridians: Feminism, Race, Transnationalism, 7*(1), 162–182. http://www.jstor.org/stable/40338721.

Robertson, I. (1987). *Sociology* (3rd. ed.). New York, NY: Worth Publishers, Inc.

Rodriguez, C. E. (2000). *Changing Race: Latinos, the Census, and the History of Ethnicity in the United States.* New York: NYU Press.

Rogers, R. (2006). *Afro-Caribbean Immigrants and the Politics of Incorporation: Ethnicity, Exception, or Exit.* Cambridge University Press.

Roth, W. (2012). *Race Migrations: Latinos and the Cultural Transformation of Race.* Stanford University Press.

Sanchez, G. R., & Morin, J. L. (2011). The Effect of Descriptive Representation on Latinos' Views of Government and of Themselves. *Social Science Quarterly, 92*(2), 483–508.

Saillant-Torres, Silvio (2000). *The Tribulations of Blackness: Stages in Dominican Racial Identity* Vol. 23, No. 3, Dominican Republic Literature and Culture (Summer, 2000). The Johns Hopkins University Press. (See pp. 1086–1111).

Serrao, Roger. (2019). "Racial Democracy" Reloaded. NACLA.

Simon, Yara. (2020). *Latino, Hispanic, Latinx, Chicano: The History Behind the Terms.* History Channel.

Skidmore, Thomas. (1992). *Black Into White Race and Nationality in Brazilian Thought.* Durham: Duke University Press.

Smith, R. M. (2004). Identities, interests, and the future of political science. *Perspectives on Politics* 2(2):301–312.

STATE OF LATINOS IN THE DISTRICT OF COLUMBIA. (2009). *Population / Economic Status / Housing / Neighborhood Change / Employment.* Jennifer Comey, Peter A. Tatian, Rosa Maria Castaneda, Michel Grosz, and Lesley Freiman. The Urban Institute Metropolitan Housing and Communities Policy Center.

Stokes-Brown, Atiya Kai. (2012). "America's Shifting Color Line? Reexamining Determinants of Latino Racial Self-Identification." *Social Science Quarterly*: 309–332

Telles, Edward, Flores D., René D., and Urrea-Giraldo, Fernando. (2015). Pigmentocracies: Educational inequality, skin color and census ethnoracial identification in eight Latin American countries. Research in Social Stratification and Mobility.

Telles, E. (2014). *Pigmentocracies: Ethnicity, Race, And Color in Latin America.* Chapel Hill: The University of North Carolina Press, Chapel Hill.

The Washington Post. (2012). Carol Morello. "Washington Area One of the Nation's Most Diverse." September.

Tuedeman, D. V. and O'Hara, R. P. (1963). *Career Development: Choice and Adjustment*. New York, NY: College Entrance Examination Board.

United States Census Bureau. (2000). https://www.census.gov/topics/population/hispanic-origin/about.html.

US Census Bureau. (2020). State and county quick facts: Race. Retrieved on March 5, 2020 from http://www.consus.gov/data.html.

Valdez, Z. (2011). Political Participation Among Latinos in the United States: The Effect of Group Identity and Consciousness. *Social Science Quarterly*, *92*(2), 466–482.

Vera, Amir and Pineda, Alexander. (2021).: *Blackness and Latinidad are not mutually exclusive. Here's what it means to be Afro-Latino in America.* CNN.

Vidal-Ortiz, Salvador and Mártinez, Juliana. (2018). "Latinx thoughts: Latinidad with an X." *Latino Studies* 16 (3): 384–395.

Wade, Peter. (2005). Rethinking Mestizaje: Ideology and Lived Experience*. *Journal of Latin American Studies 27, 238–257.*

Wahlke, John. C. (1971). Policy Demands and System Support: The Role of the Represented. *British Journal of Political Science*. Vol. 1. No. 3, 271–290).

Winter, H. R. and Bellows, T. J. (1985). *People and Politics*. 3rd ed. New York, NY: John Wiley and Sons.

Index

Page reference for figures are italicized.

A.

Action structure, 80
African Americans, 86
Afrohispano, 6, 90
Afro-Latino/a identity, 30–33
Afro-Latino/a identity in the Americas and U.S., 30, 92
Alexander, Amanda, 2
Art, 66

B.

Background entailments, 13
Black, 21, 35, 37, 47–48, 70
Blackness, 47, 63, 70
Black Latino, 63
Black lives matter, 84
Bowser, Muriel, 19, 69

C.

Campaign finance, 88
Career decision identity, 55, See also seven stages, 55–56
Centralized representation, 78
Characterization of being Afro-Latino/a, 6, 90
Colorism, 4
Colorism in the Afro-Latino/a community, 22–23
Competing perspective, 25
Comprehensive representation, 79
Conclusion, 92
Constituent theory of representation, 76
Coordinated representation, 78
Correspondence theory of representation, 76

D.

DC Afro-Latino caucus, 67
Descriptive representation, 40–41
Descriptive representation and electability of dark-skin, 38, 92
Descriptive and explanator case study, 6–8, 91
District of Columbia, 3
Dimensions of representation, 45–47
Double-consciousness, 18

E.

Ed. 61–62, 86
Ed.C, 82–83

Electability, 44, 87
Espaillat, Adriano, 22
Ethnicity, 25–29; 34–36,
Ethnicities of Latin America,
    15–18, identity, 39, 52; ethnic-racial group, 41
External representation, 74

F.

False consciousness, 8
Figure 0.1: Conceptual framework, 7, Figure 1.1: Hispanic racial demographics, *20*;
Figure 1.2: Racial demographics *21*
Fenty, Adrian, 2
Formalistic representation, 45
Freyre, Gilberto, 2, 8
Functional Theory of Representation, 77

G.

Garcia, John A., 38
Gates, Jr., Henry Louis, 33
Group identity, 57–59

H.

Hobbesian Theory on representation, 74
Hypotheses, 5

I.

Identity, 52–54
Identity politics, 38, 52, 86
Incentive, 72
Internal representation, 74

J.

Jen, 84–85
Jun, 69

K.

Khibutz, 53–54

L.

Latino/a elected officials, 49
Liability, 63
Lipschutz, Alejandro, 13
Lockean theory of representation, 75
Location matters, 82
Lopez, Jose M., 2

M.

Ma, 63–64
Marie, 68–69
Man, 70, 81–82
Mayor's office on Latino Affairs, 2, 69
Monopolistic representation, 78
Money whitens, 48

N.

National association for the advancement of colored people (NAACP), 62
Nationality, 5
Nel, 65–66, 83
Non-support from Latino/a representatives, 88

O.

Obama, Barack, 51, 87
Organization of american states, 68
One drop rule, 36, 44, 86–87

P.

Pan-ethnic group consciousness, 42
Pathway to political office, 73
Pew research center, 31
Pigmentocracy, 3, 13, 88
Pigmentocracy's impact on the opportunity, 6–8, 90
Policy recommendations, 94–95

Politics of ethnicity versus nationalism in the U.S., 6–8, 90
Political office, 39, 49
Political representation, 44, 91
Political underrepresentation, 89

Q.

Qualitative method, 10; results, 61–70

R.

Racial democracy, 2–3, 8–9
Representative, 73
Rob, 66–67
Ro, 66
Roman, Miriam Jimenez, 15
Ros, 67, 84
Rousseaunian theory of representation, 75

S.

Saillant, Silvio Torres, 34
Secondary data, 91
Skin-color, 14, 35–36, 42–44, 72, 81, 83, 87
Specialized representation, 79
Substantive representation, 45
Summary, 89

Symbolic representation, 45
Symbolic theory of representation, 75

T.

Table 1.1: Ethnic composition, *18*; Table 3.1: Interview participants, *71*.
Telles, Edward, 30
Typology of representation, 78

U.

Urbina, Ricardo, 2
U.S. census bureau, 20
U.S. house of representatives, 21

V.

Views regarding ethnicity and pigmentocracy in the Latino community, 34, 92
Voting, 43
Voter turnout, 88

W.

Wade, Peter, 33–34
Washington, DC, 3
White latino/a, 81–82
World War I, 80

About the Author

Isreal G. Mallard is graduate of Howard University and earned his Ph.D. in Political Science with a concentration in American Government, International Relations, and Comparative Politics. His research focuses on Political Representation, Ethnicity, and Afro-Latino/a Affairs in the United States as well as Colombia, Cuba, and Dominican Republic. As a researcher living in Santo Domingo, Dominican Republic, he studied the Spanish Caribbean culture, political science, and Afro-Latino/a affairs at the Pontificia Universidad Católica Madre y Maestra. He received his B.B.A. in Marketing from Jarvis Christian College. Mallard earned his M.P.A. in International Relations from the Barbara Jordan-Mickey Leland School of Public Affairs, Texas Southern University and studied Comparative Development and International Diplomacy at the University of Dar Es Salaam in Dar es Salaam, Tanzania. Before starting his 15-year career in the executive branch, he worked as a congressional staffer on Capitol Hill in Washington, DC. Mallard currently serves as a Human Resources Specialist for the U.S. Department of Transportation, works as an independent researcher in Afro-Latino/a Affairs, and is a member of the DC Afro-Latino Caucus.

www.ingramcontent.com/pod-product-compliance
Lightning Source LLC
Chambersburg PA
CBHW020128010526
44115CB00008B/1027